Treasures from the Dark

By Dr. Dwight "Ike" Reighard

Treasures from the Dark

Dark

**A book for every person
who has lost a loved one...**

By Dr. Dwight "Ike" Reighard

Foreword by Zig Ziglar

Published in the United States of America by
Quantum Leap Publications.

ISBN:1-888237-16-3

To Robin, Abigail, and Danielle.

Table of Contents

Thanks To. . .

Because this book is a slice of my life there are a number of people I want to thank for their contributions.

Ernest and Ruthie Reighard, my parents; Ramona and Judy, my sisters; and Sonny, my brother for providing me with a fun-filled home that loved and cared about people.

Robert and Nancy Covington—for becoming not only my second set of parents, but my faithful friends and supporters of my ministry.

Jay Strack   for being there for me and for encouraging me to put my story into writing.

Rick Stanley—for his hours of patient listening when I was hurting and for exhorting me to do my best.

Larry Wynn—for always believing in me, even when I didn't believe in myself.

Rodney Schell—for being the "friend that sticketh closer than a brother."

Ron Braund—who invested time and talent in helping restore me in my broken world, and who critiqued our writing.

New Hope Baptist Church—the greatest church anyone could ever hope to pastor. They've held me up by their prayers and support.

Martha Maughon—to whom I owe the greatest gratitude for the book. Anyone who knows me knows that I'm a preacher, not a writer. But she reached into my heart and put what was there on the printed page.

Al Holley—for being the friend who was always able to see positive things in me that I couldn't see in myself.

John Yarborough—who, along with Cindy, taught me that Jesus Christ could live in my heart.

Foreword

When I was a child, my mother frequently said, "All's well that ends well." I believe there is a considerable amount of truth and hope in that observation. As you read *Treasures From the Dark*, I'm certain you will have many questions in your mind about why such an event, so painfully described by Dr. Reighard, could take place. Chances are excellent that you will question God about how He could have let such a thing happen. You might even wonder if, in this case, God did make a mistake.

Treasures From the Dark gives you a unique opportunity to see the hurt and bewilderment of a man in love with his Lord as he suffered the inexpressible grief of losing the wife he loved and the baby he cherished. You'll feel his grief in a real and personal way, and you will probably shed some tears as you read about his deep, personal loss. However, as an elderly minister so eloquently put it, "It's Friday. . . but Sunday's coming!" Surely there's never been a darker moment in human history than the Friday our Lord was crucified; and just as surely, there's never been a more glorious moment than the Sunday when He arose from the dead.

In an intimate, personal, yet exhilarating way, Ike Reighard will lead you to rejoice as God works in his life to bring about the healing which only the Lord can do. You'll share some of Ike's doubts, but you'll also sense the surge of hope and joy as God brings him together with a woman whose loss had been so similar to his own. You'll thrill with the rebirth of love, gratitude, and optimism when these two move beyond their grief in a joyful and exciting way to be made one in Christ. You'll praise God as He blesses their marriage and ministry to make their life one of the truly beautiful Christian love stories of our time.

Here's a book for the hurting who are seeking hope based on spiritual truths. *Treasures From the Dark* will take you to the depths, but even there, God makes His presence felt and assures you that you're there for just a brief tour and not a permanent stay. You will be lifted to unparalleled heights. Your faith in an all-powerful, all-loving God will become more real than ever. Skillfully and sensitively presented, this message will strengthen your faith, renew your hope, and provide you with some spiritual guidelines that will make a difference in your life.

Zig Ziglar

I will give you the treasures of darkness,
And hidden riches of secret places,
That you may know that I, the Lord,
Who call you by your name,
Am the God of Israel.
Isaiah 45:3

Introduction

Dag Hammarskjold once said that the longest road is the road inward. All of us who have ever traveled that introspective road know that Hammarskjold's statement is true, for it requires our willingness to turn the pockets of our souls inside out. The journey I've made inside myself for the writing of these pages has been long and sometimes painful. But it has forced me to examine some negative emotions that might have otherwise gone unattended. For this reason, I have benefited from the endeavor far more than anyone else will.

I do not attempt to chronicle my personal strength and success here, but in the knowledge of my weakness, to declare with Charles Spurgeon, "God is too good to be unkind, and He is too wise to be mistaken. When we cannot trace His hand, we can always trust His heart." This book is simply an account of how God worked in my life.

Writing autobiographically has humbled me and increased my wonder at God's faithfulness in the events that make up my story. Though I have not lived a long time compared to many, I know the pain of struggling through fear, loneliness, grief, and depression. I have been caught in some of life's bleak and narrow passages. And I have seen God's divine genius consummate the impossible.

I believe a time comes for some of us when the scroll of His will dictates that we write a statement concerning our particular faith experience. . . a time when He asks us to share how He walked with us in the shadows, met our deepest needs, and gave us treasures out of the darkness. For me that time is now.

It is my prayer that you will see Him as you read this work which I offer to Him in grateful praise—and to you in His love.

Chapter 1
I Wish You Didn't Need to Read This Book

As a speaker, I'm always happy for people to come hear me. And as a writer, I'm glad when they pick up one of my books because they hope it will speak to their hearts. I only wish you didn't need to read this particular book. I wish you didn't feel the gnawing pain of losing someone you love, but I can't spare you that pain. I can only hope that by sharing my experiences, you will feel understood and comforted. You may not be able to fathom it now, but some day, you will look back and realize God has led you through this dark time.

When the Nazis rolled across Western Europe in the first years of World War II, country after country fell to German domination. Soon, people in those countries realized the rumors were true: Jews, other "undesirables," and anyone who helped these misfits were being shipped off to concentration camps. Corrie ten Boom heard about Ravensbrook and Auschwitz. She told her father, "Papa, I'm afraid. I don't think I could live through anything so horrible."

Her father tried to reassure her, "Yes, you could, Corrie. God would give you the grace to endure."

Corrie argued, "No, Papa. I couldn't. It is too terrible to even imagine."

Her father paused for a moment, then he asked her, "Corrie, when I take you to the train station to go visit your grandmother, do I give you the money for the fare a year ahead of time?"

She shook her head, "No, Papa."

"Do I give it to you a month ahead of time?"

"No, sir."

"A week?"

"No."

"Do I give it to you a day before you go?"

Her eyes began to brighten. "No, Papa. You give it to me the day I leave. . . the day I need it."

Her father smiled, "That's the way God's grace is, Corrie. He gives it when we need it. His grace is sufficient for the moment."

Sometimes we hear of people who go through tragedies, and we think, "There's no way I could go through something like that!" And we tell ourselves that we could never endure the pain of tragic loss. But that's simply not true. When the time comes, we can endure because God will pour out His grace on us. You may feel His grace as an incredible warmth of His presence. I remember when my wife Cindy and our baby died in 1983, I was so aware that people's prayers were lifting me to the loving hand of the Father.

But sometimes, it seems like God resides in a different time zone. In the first hours after Cindy died, I felt somebody had injected novocaine in my soul. I was absolutely numb. I thought it was only a bad—no, a terrible—dream. I kept thinking I would wake up and Cindy would walk through the door again. Then, after the funeral service was over, after the family and friends had left, and after the last of the food people had brought was eaten or thrown out, I took a deep breath and looked around at the empty cavern of our—no, my—now silent house. For the first time in many years, I couldn't hear Cindy's voice or feel her next to me. I felt so alone. So helpless. So abandoned.

One of the most encouraging passages of the Bible is in Psalm 73. The writer, Asaph, is really discouraged. He, too, feels like God has let Him down, and he's angry at God. Does he feel "the warmth of God's presence"? No way! But then he reflects:

When my heart was grieved
and my spirit embittered,
I was senseless and ignorant;
I was a brute beast before you."

Have you felt like that? I sure have. Sometimes I was
so angry and sad! But there's a transition word next in
the passage that changes everything: "yet."

Yet I am always with you;
you hold me by my right hand.
You guide me with your counsel,
and afterward you will take me into glory. . . .
My flesh and my heart may fail,
but God is the strength of my heart
and my portion forever"
(Psalm 73:21-26).

Asaph was saying, "When I was at my worst, God
reached out and took my hand. He didn't recoil and tell
me to 'Shape up!' He tenderly led me through the valley
. . . even when I didn't even know He was there." We may
feel alone sometimes, but we can be sure that God is with
us in His tenderness, wisdom, and strength.

When we are faced with the death of someone we
love, it's easy to get confused and discouraged. Many of
us are conscientious Christians. We love God, and we
trust Him, and we mistakenly think God should put up
a plexi-glass shield around us to protect us from anything really painful. When we come face to face with
death, we say to Him, "Why in the world did You let this
happen, God?! You are sovereign. You could have prevented it!"

It's one thing to *hear* a sermon or a story of how
someone dealt with the death of a spouse or a parent or
a child, but it's quite another thing to now *live* the story.
The pain is so real, so close, so overwhelming, you can't
imagine you will ever get over it. But with some help, you
can grieve the deep sense of loss and find strength and
hope again.

In our society, we are surprised by death. Modern

medicine has made great advances. Only a few genera-
tions ago, half of all people died by the age of five. These
modern advances have deceived us (or we have deceived
ourselves) to think we can somehow cheat death—but
death is inevitable. It captures every single person, and
it touches every life. Death is the unwelcomed guest that
knocks at every door, often at the most unexpected
times. At that moment, emotions flood in. We feel betrayed, afraid, and angry at the injustice of death stealing someone so precious from us. We feel disillusioned
that God would treat us so badly when we have served
Him so faithfully. Haven't we followed the narrow path?
Haven't we built our house upon a rock? Haven't we
forsaken all to follow Him? Don't we deserve better? But
the rain (and the sleet and hail) falls on the just and the
unjust alike.

  Some of us assume that we've done something so bad
that God is paying us back by causing this death. One of
the first things that runs through our minds is: "I must
have done something. It must be my fault." We think of
David committing adultery with Bathsheba. God allowed the child they conceived to die. We wonder, "Okay,
what did I do that caused God's judgment?" Or maybe we
feel guilty about what we didn't do: "What did I fail to do
that led to this person's death?" I try to remind people
that if God wanted to teach you a lesson, he doesn't have
to go through another person to get your attention. He
will speak directly to you!

  People with different temperaments handle grief in
different ways. People who are outgoing and optimistic
often get very busy. They try to fill up their lives with
people and activities to do so they won't have to feel the
pain. Reflective people often withdraw into a shell and
become very pensive and sad. They think and feel deeply
about the loss, and usually need some encouragement to
get out and get going again. People who are organized
and detailed often think they could have done "just one
more thing" and prevented the death. They lament, "I
should have seen this coming. I *should have* planned
better." They are often consumed with guilt for not doing
enough, even though they did all that could possibly be

done for that person. The tough, decisive people just get angry—at the person for dying, at the doctors and nurses for not doing enough, at other family members for crying so much, and at themselves (though they may not admit it) for feeling so helpless.

Some of us are prone to depression because we feel so deeply. Others don't allow themselves to feel deeply enough. They try to get rid of the bad feelings as soon as possible. It's helpful to understand how our own temperament affects how we handle loss, and we also need to understand how other family members tend to respond so we won't get so impatient with them. Now, more than ever, we need each others' empathy and compassion—not criticism for not grieving the "right" way, our way.

Of course, there's no shortage of people who will tell you how you should grieve. One person will tell how she handled her mother's death; another will give you an article out of a magazine; somebody else will talk about her deep grief when her dog died; and others will give that always helpful advice: "Just get over it!" Thanks a lot!

People who are quick to offer you advice about grief probably haven't dealt with their own very well. Some believe that "getting over it" means you completely forget that person. You will always have memories of that person—the good times and the bad—unless you have a lobotomy! When an athlete recovers from a severe injury and goes back to playing the game, he always has that injury in the back of his mind. He has felt the pain, he has struggled through rehab, and he is a stronger person for having gone through that process. The athlete lives with the memory of pain, and now he knows how to comfort and encourage other athletes who get injured.

Some of us experience the sudden shock of a quick impact death, and we are left feeling terribly fragile. We think, "All it takes is one phone call, and my life goes to pieces. All it takes is one knock on the door with somebody standing there saying, 'I regret to inform you. . . .' and the world comes to an end again." Some of us live with that nagging fear. Every day my children get out of the car when I take them to school and I watch them walk away, I am aware—painfully aware—that this could be the last time I ever see them. Every day of my life I think of how fragile life is. You see, when I took Cindy to the hospital that day to have our child, I was ready for one of the happiest days of my life. We live in a world of modern medicine, incredible technology, and complete confidence, but all of a sudden, those most dear to me were dead. Dead. What an awful word. It just couldn't be happening! But it was. In a moment, my heights of joyful anticipation were crushed into the dark, ugly, empty hole of despair. I realized my life would never be the same. I felt completely hopeless and helpless. The only thing I could do was pray... but God didn't answer my prayers (at least, not the way I wanted Him to).

I recently heard of a family in Texas whose 14 year-old daughter was kidnapped, raped, and murdered. I can't imagine a more horrible thing to happen—to that precious young girl or to her parents. When Cindy died, I at least stood in that room and saw those doctors and nurses try everything possible to save Cindy and the baby. I saw tears stream down their faces when they turned to me and said it was over. They were not coldly professional. These men and women were brokenhearted when my wife and child's lives faded away. If a death surrounded by competence and care devastated me, how awful it must be to have a family member or friend die at the hands of a criminal in a senseless act.

A friend of mine and his wife were missionaries in Africa. They had a flat tire when they were traveling back from a speaking engagement, and some men stopped behind them. These men grabbed my friend and beat his wife to death. He had to cope with intense anger toward these men. Some might want to tell him, "Brother, anger is sin." Well, let me tell you, that probably wouldn't help him a whole lot! In those situations, anger is a reality. Most Christians have a very simplistic view of anger. The fact is, the feeling of anger isn't sin. In Ephesians 4, Paul instructs us to "be angry." But angry feelings can lead to angry actions. Taking revenge is sin. It is destructive for all involved. People who have lost loved ones to criminal acts or negligence will feel anger. They shouldn't try to stuff it, instead, they need to channel it toward positive, healthy actions.

Many couples experience the pain of miscarriage. Their grief is often minimized by others who can't understand their loss. These observers might say, "Well, you never had the child, so your loss can't be that bad!" But I assure you, it is. The anticipation of having that baby, the eager longing to hold him, the deep desire to watch her grow to maturity—make losing the child a deep wound. From the day Cindy and I learned she was pregnant, I lay my head on her stomach and prayed for our baby every night. We had wanted a child for so long, but we had been unable to have one. Now, finally, God had answered our prayers! That child was dear to both of us before we ever saw him. And that child was dear to God, too. The Bible says that if there is a physical body, there is a spirit. When we get to heaven, a lot of us are going to meet our children who died before or during birth. I believe they are there waiting for us. That gives me comfort.

Husbands often minimize their wife's grief in miscarriage for a couple of reasons. The mother has carried that child, felt the kicks and daydreamed about nurturing that precious baby in the coming years, so she has a more natural bond with the child. And women are simply more sensitive than men. They tend to feel things more deeply, so they are more apt to be devastated by the loss of the child—and by a spouse's lack of appropriate grief over the death.

Men, however, may not actually minimize the loss. They may just not feel comfortable talking about it. Men are task-oriented. They set goals, and they overcome obstacles. The sooner the better! Getting over a death is a goal to many men, and they try to put it behind them as quickly and as painlessly as possible. That doesn't do them much good, and it certainly doesn't help them relate to others in the family who struggle through the grieving process. Women are process-oriented. They grieve by talking to their friends, and these friends know they don't have to give answers to fix them. They only need to listen and provide a shoulder to cry on. Men think, "What's talking about it going to accomplish? It's not going to change what happened." Men live by agendas, goals, tasks. Women live by relationships. They don't need (or want) answers. They need intimacy. For this reason, many men have a very difficult time dealing with death because they don't really allow themselves to go through the grief process. The macho image doesn't lend itself to dealing with a deep wound. (These are the usual ways men and women respond to loss, but of course, there are exceptions. I know men who are very sensitive and talk freely about their pain, and I know women who try to be tough and act like their tragic losses don't really bother them.)

One of the mistakes we make is to compare our losses. We may think—and we may even say—"My loss is worse than yours." But can anybody say that my losing my wife is easier or harder than Cindy's mother and father losing their daughter? Or Cindy's sister who lost her best friend and sister? When Cindy died, I was absolutely devastated. Losing a spouse is one of the most traumatic events anybody can endure. But so is losing a child. Or a parent. Everybody's pain is overwhelming and real to them, and every relationship is unique, lovely, and valuable. Maybe we want to think that somehow the incredible pain we feel makes us superior to others in some way, but that is foolish and wrongheaded. Or perhaps we feel the need to minimize our own pain and say that others' hurts are far deeper and more devastating. Neither of these is appropriate, and neither is helpful. Don't compare your hurt to anybody else's.

One of the most difficult things to face is to watch the health of a person you love slowly deteriorate, day after day, week after week, month after month, year after year. In those times, we realize there is something worse than death. As painful as this time is, it at least allows the family and friends to prepare for the eventual death. You have the opportunity to plan for the funeral, and you have the chance to say "goodbye." Those who lose someone in a crisis long for one more moment to say "I love you" one more time, or to say "Please forgive me" and clear up some unfinished business, or just to hold that person one more time. A sudden death shocks those left behind, and a long, lingering death requires those who care to grieve a little day after day even before the person dies. Sometimes the greatest prayer you can utter for someone is not, "Please, God, let him live," but "Please, God, let him die so his suffering can end."

Years ago I came across a letter Benjamin Franklin wrote to a lady named Elizabeth Hubbard to comfort her in her grief. It was penned on February 22, 1756. Franklin's words provide insight, perspective, and hope:

Dear Child,

I condole with you. We have lost a most dear and valuable relation, but it is the will of God and nature that these mortal bodies be laid aside, when the soul is to enter into real life; it's rather an embryo state, a preparation for living.

A man is not completely born until he is dead. Why then should we grieve that a new child is born among the immortals? A new member added to their happy family? That bodies should be lent us is a kind and benevolent act of God.

When they become unfit for these purposes and afford us pain instead of pleasure—instead of an aid, become an incumbrance and answer non of the intentions for which they were given— it is equally kind and benevolent that a way is provided by which we may get rid of them. Death is that way.

We ourselves often prudently choose a partial death. In some cases a mangled limb, which cannot be restored, is willingly cut off. He who plucks out a tooth parts with it freely, since the pain goes with it; and thus a person surrenders the whole body, and departs at once, for with it goes all pain and possibilities of pain, all diseases and suffering.

Thus, we are invited abroad on a party of pleasure that is to last forever. Perhaps, a loved

one has gone before us. We could not all conve-
niently start together, and why should we be
grieved at this, since we are soon to follow,
and we know where to find him or her.
    Benjamin Franklin

There is hope—great hope!—of being with our loved
one again "on the other side." And in that, we are
comforted. And even if we are not sure of how the one we
love responded to Christ, we can know that God sometimes works at the last minute, like the thief on the cross,
in His infinite mercy. The God I believe in is not trying
to keep people out of heaven. He sent His own dear Son
to die for each of us, and He dearly wants each person to
trust Him and spend eternity in His presence. That, too,
gives us hope.

If you are in the midst of the grief process, I want to
assure you, things will get better. It is not that "time
heals all wounds." It doesn't. But time gives you the
opportunity to talk, to reflect, to feel angry and sad, and
to allow God, family and friends to be a part of your
healing process. The greatest hope we have is that death
is not the end. There is another life. When I stand in front
of a casket with a family and we know that person was
a believer, I can say with absolute certainty, "Your
father (or mother or husband or wife or child or friend)
is just as alive as we are. He's in another place, but he's
alive." I believe that sometimes God pulls back the veil
and allows "the great cloud of witnesses" to peer over the
parapets of heaven to see what we're doing down here.
Our loved ones are our cheerleaders! Sometimes I think
of some dear people who are there in heaven watching
me as I try to walk with God, and I know they are pulling
for me. That gives me great comfort and encouragement.

Grief is a refining process. It's not pleasant, but it's
effective. It can mark one of the most important transitions in your life as God uses that time to redirect your
priorities and deepen your walk with Him. It is a time to
evaluate what really matters—and what doesn't. One of
the biggest steps a person makes is when they stop
saying "why?" and they start saying "what now?" The

questions become: "What can I learn? How can I use what I've been through to help other people?" Adversity is God's way of preparing you to help others, and in fact, I believe it is only those who have endured adversity who can genuinely help other people. Paul wrote about this in his second letter to the Christians in Corinth: "Praise be to the God and Father of our Lord Jesus Christ, the Father of compassion and the God of all comfort, who comforts us in all our troubles, so that we can comfort those in any trouble with the comfort we ourselves have received from God. For just as the sufferings of Christ flow over into our lives, so also through Christ our comfort overflows" (II Corinthians 1:3-5). You see, it is we who have suffered and experienced comfort who have the ability to truly comfort others. I'm sure you can tell that is true already. Those who "have all the answers" and try to fix you leave you feeling cold and empty, but those who have been in the crucible and come through it know they don't have to have all the answers. They only need to be there alongside to offer hope, love, and support. In the grieving process, you, too, will learn to empathize with others, so you can say quietly to others who hurt, "I understand. I've been there."

The struggle of grief will also refine you. Wrestling with the loss actually becomes a catharsis, a release of the deep hurts and a capturing of new hope. Don't try to bypass this struggle. It will make you a stronger person by burning away the dross in your life. The struggle will enable you to gain a deeper, fuller understanding of what life's about. Job said, "I will be tried, and when I come forth, I'll be purer than gold." No, nobody in his right mind would choose the path of grief as a course in spiritual growth! But someone has chosen it for you, and he is called "Lord," "Master," and "Father."

I want you to know that I've been thinking of you. I've thought of your pain, your loneliness, your sense of guilt and anger, and your need to feel loving arms around you. Before you read further in this book, I want to pray for you.

Heavenly Father, I want to pray for this dear friend reading these words. Lord, You know what happened,

and You care. In the middle of all the heartache, help this
dear person sense a deep, strong hope that comes from
Jesus Christ. We may not understand why we experience this kind of loss, but I pray this friend will choose
to become better and not bitter. Instead of becoming cold
and cynical, grant a heart of compassion and caring.
Don't let us waste our grief. Show us a way we can turn
what seems so terrible at this moment into a trophy.
God, I know You can do that by Your amazing grace.
Strengthen this dear person. Give hope in the present so
we can have power in the future. Grant Your grace which
is totally sufficient for any problem and any need. Lord,
You did that for me, and I know You'll make this a reality
for this friend, too. In Jesus' strong name, Amen.

Chapter 2
"Oh, Cindy"

When the words, "Code one hundred to labor and delivery!" blasted through the intercom at Piedmont Hospital, I ran toward Cindy's room. By some revelation, I knew that emergency alarm signaled trouble for my wife.

Doctors and nurses came from everywhere. Someone shoved a crash cart into Cindy's room. Strangers in green scrub clothes pushed past me as I forced my way in.

"Out of the way!" a voice snapped.

"Get out of the room," another ordered.

"That's my wife!" I snapped back. "I'm staying with her."

Cindy needed me. I desperately wanted to get near her. If I could just take her hand, hold her, she would be all right. But I moved back obediently and watched in stunned disbelief the tragedy unfolding before me.

Only moments earlier, Cindy had been vibrant and smiling as she sent me to tell our family and friends in the waiting room that her pain had eased and it wouldn't be long until the baby would be here. Now she lay motionless as specialists worked feverishly to revive her. I stared at her heart monitor, refusing its declaration that Cindy was in cardiac arrest.

A team of Emory University heart surgeons—

among the best in the country—were in a teaching session on another floor. Responding to the emergency call, they came within minutes. Cindy's gown was stripped off and her chest repeatedly compressed.

One doctor whirled around to ask me, "Do you want us to save your wife or your child?"

"My wife, my wife! Please save my wife."

The signal on the baby's heart monitor flattened. In terror, I jammed my body against the wall for support and begged God to intervene.

Trained hands placed defibrillator paddles over Cindy's heart. Someone counted off seconds while the machine charged. I heard scraps of talk.

"Stand back!"

"Clear!"

A dull thud—the shock to Cindy's heart. Her body tightened, then flopped on the bed like a rag doll.

The life color slowly paled from her legs and arms. As an ominous blue crept over her body, a dark blanket of guilt began to cover me. Why had I wanted a baby? It had been far too important to me. I had done this terrible thing to Cindy. *Oh, God, have I killed her?*

I shivered as a chilling wind seemed to rustle through me, leaving me cold and alone. At that moment something inside me silently left its dwelling place. I knew Cindy was dying.

Two nurses led me into the hall. They held my hands. . . literally held me up. A hospital chaplain joined us.

"She's dead, isn't she!?" I asked.

"No, not yet," he responded quietly.

"Please, don't lie to me!"

"I'm not," he tried to reassure me. "They've got a heartbeat, but they can't keep her blood pressure up. They're doing everything they can."

For what seemed an eternity, I stared hopelessly into the arena that held the fate of the one dearest to me in all the world.

Dr. Neal Newsome, Cindy's obstetrician, arrived as quickly as possible and hurried into her room. After what seemed like hours, he came out. As he approached me, I read the final truth in his face.

"It's over, isn't it?" I asked.

"Yes, we've been working on her for about fifty minutes now. Ike, I'm sorry. I'm sorry." He looked at me through tear-blurred eyes and spoke with a quiver in his voice. "Everything possible has been done for her."

"I know, I know," I said, embracing him. I wanted to comfort him, to let him know that I didn't blame him. He was more than a doctor. He had become a good friend, a fellow-Christian who loved Cindy too.

I stepped inside the door of Cindy's room. The activity had slowed, but a few doctors and nurses were still with her. The best that medical science could offer had proven inadequate. The machines offended me now. "Get the tubes off of her," I choked. "Get 'em all off! Please, just leave her alone." Gently, they pulled the sheet over Cindy's face.

They trailed out of the room looking like defeated warriors returning from battle. Their eyes, filled with tears, were set in grieved faces.

A nurse handed me Cindy's jewelry—her wedding band, her watch, an anniversary ring, and a bracelet. "Where's the snowflake?" I asked, referring to a necklace I'd given Cindy for our tenth Christmas together. It was a cluster of small diamonds in the form of a snowflake, mounted in yellow gold. I'd chosen its design because Cindy, like each snowflake, was one of a kind. The diamonds reflected the sparkle of her personality. She had loved it, and its meaning made the necklace special to both of us.

I began to search the room for it. I couldn't find it at first. I checked the bed, night table, and the floor around the bed. I got down on my hands and knees and crawled around until I finally spotted the necklace in a corner. The chain was broken. Obviously, it had been torn from Cindy's neck and flung across the room during the emergency. I picked it up and turned it toward the light. It looked strangely different. The sparkle was gone. Was it because of my tears? Or had the diamonds symbolically lost their luster?

Standing so near to Cindy, I couldn't help but pull

back the cover to look at her once more. How tiny and fragile she looked there on the sterile sheets of the foreboding hospital bed. So still and lifeless, she didn't seem like my Cindy. The sharp sword of reality stabbed my heart.

"Oh, Cindy! How could you possibly die?!"

I smoothed her hair, then bent down and kissed her unresponsive lips. I grasped her hand, but she did not grasp mine in return. Only moments before we had been excited and happy, watching a dream come true. Suddenly the mysterious outrage of death had torn her from me, and for the first time I understood the deeper meaning of "two shall become one."

My thoughts were interrupted by Dr. Newsome. "Are you ready to tell her family now?" I needed a few minutes to get myself together. How could I break the soul-crushing news to Cindy's mom and dad?

"I am a minister of the gospel of Jesus Christ," I said to the doctor. "With all my heart, I believe that Cindy is with Him now. But I know that's not going to stop the shock and pain for her family."

I had a flashing memory of asking Cindy once if she had ever doubted her salvation. When she said, "No," I had pushed a little.

"Not ever?"

"No, Ike." She had been emphatic. "When I was a little girl, my daddy led me to Christ. I clearly remember that he knelt with me as I asked Jesus to come into my heart. I even remember what I was wearing, and I remember how Daddy's hand felt on mine. It was real and I've never doubted it."

I had to tell this father that his child had gone to be forever with the Savior they shared.

Resolutely, I made my way through the double doors out of labor and delivery and into the room where friends and family waited anxiously. They already knew that the emergency activity had been on Cindy's behalf. Now they must be told that it had ended in her death.

"I'm sorry, I'm sorry," my voice broke. In my passionate effort to tell them what happened, I was finally able to cry.

"Oh, God, not my baby!" Cindy's mother sobbed. I searched the eyes of my father-in-law with a new sense of fraternity—I had lost a child. So had he.

"It can't be true!" Cindy's sister Becky protested.

Friends who had come for the joy of the day moaned in disbelief. "Oh no. . . . Oh no!"

Rodney Schell, one of my fellow ministers at New Hope Baptist Church and close as a brother to Cindy and me, stood by in those dreadful moments. I saw in him a strength I would need in the weeks and months to follow.

The doctors came to speak with us, explaining in solemn tones all they knew. Cindy had suffered cardiac arrest, her lungs quit functioning, her respiratory system stopped. . . and she was gone.

Later, we were told that she died of an amniotic fluid embolism, a phenomenon about which medical science knows very little since there are not enough cases on record to permit adequate study. Only one mother out of thousands encounters amniotic fluid embolism, and rarely is one stricken before reaching the stage of delivery. Why Cindy?

The doctors' heart-twisting questions needed answers. An autopsy? No. Remove the baby from the mother's womb? No, leave it with her. They belong together. A funeral director was called and Cindy's body was taken away. There was nothing left to do but go home.

Another good friend, Al Holley, guided me down the long hospital corridors and out of the building to his car. He didn't say much as he drove along, but I could tell he was hurting too. . . sharing the pain of a buddy. Somehow that helped.

As we drove out of Atlanta on Interstate 75 that warm spring evening, the sun was setting. It dropped behind the jagged line of the tallest buildings, spreading glorious hues of crimson and gold across the sky.

Early evening had always been my favorite time of day. Cindy had loved it too. We were both home- and family-oriented, and sunset called us to gather ourselves home. Countless times we had stood together on our porch and marveled at the greatness of God at sunset.

Only He could unfurl such brilliant colors across the sky, then fade them into velvety folds of dusty pink and grey . . . and command them differently every time His sun went down.

My fondness for this time of day must have begun in childhood. I remembered hearing my mother call me to bring down my kite and head for home—home where a warm supper and a happy, laughing family waited.

No longer would sunset speak to me of warmth and happiness. Numbly, I laid my head against the headrest in the car and closed my eyes. Surely I would wake up in a minute and find none of this was real. It had to be just a terrible dream!

As we reached the Atlanta airport area, great expanses of sky opened before us. The last bit of color had faded. Deep shadows of sadness and fear stole over me like the unbridled night.

Once again it was time to bring down the kite, time to go home, time for the family to gather in. . . .

But not tonight. Home would not be home, because only a part of me would be there.

Chapter 3

Please Don't Turn Out the Light

That trip home was the longest I've ever taken. As we rounded a curve on Stanley Road about seven o'clock in the evening, the sight of our home deepened my pain, already too heavy to bear.

Cindy and I had been in our new home for only three months. We'd never owned a home of our own before. We had so much fun designing, planning, selecting. . . doing all the things that go into building a house. Built in a Tudor style with a centerpiece turret, it looked a little like the castle I'd promised Cindy. It was a good thing Al was driving that night. I could have never deliberately directed the car up the driveway to that empty house with its pernicious reminders.

I went in through the garage and forced myself to put my key in the back door lock and turn. As I opened the door and stepped into the kitchen, a grim, unseen hand reached into my chest and pulled my heart up through my throat. My stomach twisted, and I felt sick. I can't stand this! There's no way I can get through it!

I became a player on a stage as I moved from the kitchen toward the hall, acting out what had to be. The scenes around me changed automatically. Zombie-like, I could neither encourage them to change nor wish them to remain the same.

The phone began to ring, and family and friends

were soon gathering. They wanted to help.

I don't want any help! Yes, yes, I do want help! Don't leave me alone. Oh, God, I just want Cindy and the baby here—the way it was supposed to be. Please, God, just help me to hang on!

I was praying but my prayers didn't seem like prayers. They were just my pleas spinning into empty air. Seemingly abandoned by God, I understood the phrase that Harold Tandrup used in his book, *Reluctant Prophet*. He said that after God had given the blunt order to Jonah, "The Lord went into His eternity and closed the door behind Him."

Filled with a melange of pain and sorrow, my first impression was to go into the nursery. I had to see the nursery. Drawn in that direction, I paused when I reached the door. There I noticed little spots from double stick tape that told the story of happy balloons hung to welcome a baby—then hurriedly snatched away. Just like my baby. Inside the room my eyes slowly scanned the perfect setting. An animal motif, with a soft aqua color. . . suitable for a boy or a girl. The room had a traditional flair with Queen Anne furniture and some white wicker accent pieces. Decorating it and shopping the antique stores for rare treasures had been so much fun. I remembered Cindy, chubby with the final months of pregnancy, bubbling about putting the stuffed toys into place. I pictured a little red-haired baby quietly sleeping in the crib, or maybe squirming on the changing table. The cruel truth landed a new blow as the sad and silent nursery mocked me. There would be no baby. Not now. . . not ever.

I turned to a couple of Cindy's closest friends and insisted, "Pack it all up and give it away. The furniture, clothes, toys, all of it. Take it away so I'll never have to see it again."

"Death devours all lovely things," Edna St. Vincent Millay once wrote. With a new assurance, I knew she was right.

Bedtime came that evening in spite of my effort to hold it back. My sister Judy went with me to the bedroom. In that barren room that had been so precious to me when Cindy was just a pillow away, I asked Judy if she would stay with me. When she agreed, I quickly added, "But please don't turn out the light." The light had gone out on so much of my life that day, I couldn't possibly face the darkness of the night. I felt that all I was enduring would somehow be more tolerable in the light. Not bothering to undress or to turn down the spread, I stretched out on the bed Cindy and I had shared. Only two nights before she was in my arms there. We had prayed together and gone to sleep. . . thinking about our baby.

What about those prayers, God? What about your promises to hear and answer?

Mentally and emotionally spent, I closed my eyes, hoping for sleep. I was like a car with engine knock. I turned off my switch, but I just kept running—just kept knocking. Cindy's face began to appear and reappear. Clearly, too clearly, I saw different expressions that had made her so unique to me.

Giving in to the remembering, I saw myself as a teenager, sitting in a classroom at O'Keefe High School in Atlanta, Georgia. Without warning, the door of that room swung open, and into view popped a cute, freckled face with a smile as big as a house. That was my introduction to Cindy Mitchell. About the size of a Duracell AAA battery, Cindy charged a room with her sunshine laughter and sparkling personality.

Her happy nature attracted me immediately and we became good friends. One day a buddy asked me to call Cindy and get him a date for the following night. When I asked her about it, she replied, "Well, I'm not going out with him at the last minute."

I liked her spunky attitude. "How'd you like to go out with me next weekend?" I ventured. She delighted me by accepting, "That sounds a lot better."

The next Friday night I took Cindy to an O'Keefe football game. As a majorette, she wore a green, sequined uniform. At halftime I watched her whirl and twirl in that shimmering green outfit with her thick, red hair flying in the wind. She looked like a Christmas tree—a splendid, happy Christmas tree! *That's for me!* I determined. *Merry Christmas!*

The sweet remembrance amused my aching heart as I tossed and turned that night. Visions of Cindy persisted. A beautiful bride walked slowly toward me. I don't know that I ever proposed to Cindy. I know I never got down on bended knee with a bouquet of flowers and said, "Cindy, will you marry me?" I think we proposed to each other. We just had the understanding that when the time was right, we would get married. The right time came in June of 1971.

I could still hear Pastor John Yarborough's words as we stood together at the altar of the First Baptist Church of Chattahoochee. "Do you, Ike Reighard, take Cindy Mitchell. . . ?" "I do," I promised, and committed all that I was or ever hoped to be. As I thought of that, every disappointment I'd ever caused her taunted me with the guilt of what I should have done.

Cindy and I embarked on a married life that was filled with learning and growing, for we were only kids just out of the nest. We often laughed and told people we married so young we couldn't decide if we wanted to go on a honeymoon or go to summer camp. Our family joke was still funny to me that night in my sadness. On an emotional roller coaster, I was smiling inside one minute; the next minute I was aching inside.

Sleep still refused to come as old scenes continued to replay in my mind.

Cindy supported and assisted me in every way she could while I went to school to prepare for the ministry. Those days were tough, especially financially. We ate a lot of Hamburger Helper and dropped in on in-laws with the frequency of unwanted bills. We wanted to live independently and with integrity, but we had their dinner schedules memorized. And God bless them, they were always gracious and generous. We ordered a lot of cokes at the Dairy Queen when we really wanted milkshakes, because we didn't have the thirty cents difference. I skipped lunch many times and bought little bouquets of flowers for Cindy. Her smile was much more satisfying than a Big Mac. I was glad now for every thoughtful thing I'd ever done for her.

But new pain arose as I thought of those Christmases when I didn't have money to buy her a nice gift. I made her little coupon books. "This coupon is good for one back rub"; "This coupon is good for one vacuuming of the house"; and so on to fill the book. She laughed and flipped through the pages, warning me that she intended to cash every one of them. And she did!

Cindy hated working away from home, but she had to in those days so we could make ends almost meet. During my first quarter of college, I dropped her off at her job on my way to school. It was wintertime and really cold. Each morning she reluctantly climbed out of the car and hesitated on the sidewalk. Her warm breath puffed visibly in the cold air as she pulled her old, brown coat around her neck against the wind. Sometimes I saw she had tears in her eyes. I tried to keep her from seeing mine as I slowly drove away.

Although she never complained, the sacrifices and uncertainties got to her sometimes. I hated myself for not providing better for her, and I looked at her and vowed with determination: "Someday I'll dress you like a queen and put you in a castle, because that's what you deserve."

Continuing to throw myself about on the bed that miserable first night without Cindy, I muttered shredded prayers.

"God, I don't want to recount all of this now. . . or maybe I do. . . ."

Chapter 4

The Man Who Had Everything

Cindy had been afraid to have a baby, yet because I wanted one, she wanted it too. We'd been married for nearly twelve years before we felt the time was right to begin our family. In the summer of 1982 when we learned that Cindy was pregnant, we were elated. I never knew a Daisy Home Test Kit could be so much fun!

The positive result from that test set me to contemplating how good God had been to me. I had a personal relationship with a loving heavenly Father; a thriving ministry with a growing, caring church; a brand new home; the world's most sensational wife; and now to crown it all, a baby on the way! Overflowing with gratitude, I considered myself to be a man who had everything.

During "our pregnant months," we acted like children with a new toy as we dreamed, prepared, and waited for Baby Reighard. Except for some morning sickness during the early weeks and a flu bug later on, Cindy felt quite good. She entered her last trimester enjoying a healthy pregnancy. I'd never seen such a happy, pregnant lady. She amplified every joy, and savored every stage, every thought, every feeling that accompanies expectant motherhood. And, although that subtle fear of childbirth underlay her anticipation, she tried never to let it show.

Cindy was in her ninth month when on Friday morning, February 25, we went to Dr. Newsome for her twelfth regular checkup. We always looked forward to seeing Dr. Newsome. He treated us kindly and spent a lot of time answering our questions and entering into our happiness. He liked to tease Cindy. He, too, had red hair, so he claimed that she had to sign a contract allowing him to keep the baby for himself if it were born with red hair.

On that Friday, however, Dr. Newsome discovered that Cindy's blood pressure was a little high. He advised her to go home, rest over the weekend, then come back on Monday so he could check her again. He added that if her blood pressure hadn't regained a more normal status by then, he might put her in the hospital and induce labor. He encouraged us not to worry. It was just something he would have to watch. Cindy spent the weekend resting at home. She lounged on the sofa while I did simple chores and kept things moving for us.

"I'm feeling great," Cindy announced on Monday morning as we prepared to leave for the doctor's office. We thought surely her blood pressure was okay. When Dr. Newsome checked her, though, it was higher than it had been on Friday. He made arrangements for her to enter Piedmont Hospital immediately. The hospital was just up the street from Dr. Newsome's office so we were there in minutes. We checked in, located Cindy's room, got her into a hospital gown, and into bed. A nurse gave her a shot for her blood pressure. We settled in and began our version of the universal baby-waiting routine.

All along I kept asking the nurses to take Cindy's blood pressure and tell me what it was. They humored me, and if they were irritated, they didn't let on. Eventually, they gave us the good news that the pressure was improving. That, coupled with the security of having her in the hospital, made us feel a little less anxious. We whiled away the afternoon watching television and talking about our favorite subject—the baby. When evening came, the nurses encouraged me to go home, explaining that Cindy and I both needed to rest. I hated to leave her but I wanted to do what was best.

About eleven o'clock I reluctantly got up to leave. I knelt beside Cindy's bed for our usual nightly prayer together. It was such a sweet time as we prayed that God would protect our child. "And God, please watch over Cindy," I added, fully believing that He would. "Because she is the most precious possession I have."

All the way home, I pondered the mystery of the birth of a baby, our baby. Maybe, by that time the next night I would be a new dad. I popped in a tape and rolled back the sunroof. Life was really great!

Cindy called me the next morning, the first day of March 1983, as we had agreed. Everything was fine. The doctor planned to watch her that day and if the baby had not come naturally, he planned to induce labor on Wednesday. I left the house for the hospital, making only one quick stop. I picked up two sausage biscuits to fill Cindy's breakfast order. She told me, "One for me and one for the baby."

At the hospital, Cindy's mother met me with instructions: "Hurry on down to Cindy, Ike. Her water broke and they've moved her to the labor room."

"Wonderful!" I exclaimed, surprised at the unexpected but much-prayed-for development. Deliriously happy, I took off down the hall carrying two sausage biscuits and a big orange drink, and swinging a camera on my arm. A pumped-up papa-to-be, I couldn't wait to put on my bona fide scrub suit and get the show on the road!

When I entered her room, Cindy's face lit up. She appeared completely oblivious to the two IV tubes in her hand, the monitors that registered her heartbeat, the fetal heartbeat, her blood pressure, and her contractions. To me she looked small and helpless surrounded by those machines, even though she was nearly nine months pregnant. Her red hair fanned out on the pillow and framed her face in the prettiest way. I was so glad to see her!

About eleven-thirty that morning, she started to have painful contractions. I guess I should say we started our painful contractions. I knew she would hurt, but that didn't make it any easier for me. When she winced, I winced. As her guardian and protector, I'd always tried to protect her from pain. And when I couldn't keep her from suffering, I suffered too.

Through the day, we reckoned together with the tedious concern of having a baby. I held her hand. Adjusted her bed. . . first up. . . then down. I gave her ice chips and placed hot towels on her stomach for the cramping. "I love you so much. I'm really proud of you for having our baby," I tried to encourage her.

She thought of lots of things I could do to help her, and we worked on into the afternoon, talking as much as we could about our future and the little one who was already such an important part of our lives.

As the nurse reported on Cindy's dilation, I would mention going out to tell waiting family and friends how she was progressing. "No, not now," she insisted every time. "I want you to stay here with me."

I left her room only once during the day. I went to the hospital cafeteria with Becky to grab a hamburger. While I was out, I bought Cindy a little, pink, stuffed rabbit. This was to be a "transition bunny." I'd heard that the transition time in labor is pretty fierce, and I thought the bunny would help me avoid getting choked! When I brought it back, she smiled, "Why'd you get pink? You know you're pulling for a little boy." She was wrong about the little boy, but I hugged her and answered, "Because the bunny is not for the baby, it's for you. I want you to hold on to it while you are going through some of your pain. Beat on the rabbit, but please don't hurt me!"

At four-thirty in the afternoon, following one of her routine checks, the nurse announced, "You've dilated quite well now and it's time to call Dr. Newsome."

Soon after that, an anesthesiologist came in. He suggested that I step outside while he gave Cindy an epidural. I didn't want to leave because she was hurting pretty badly, but I told her to hold on to her bunny, and I would be right back.

When I returned, Cindy had a radiantly happy expression rather than the tired, strained one she had worn for the past several hours. "Oh, Ike, this epidural is wonderful. I don't feel any more pain. The nurse told me I've dilated even more and everything is going fine. It won't be long now, and I feel so good!" Then she said something that she had not said all day. "Go back and tell Mother, Dad, and the others that I'm not hurting now. Tell them I'm okay."

"Cindy, I'm so glad you're not hurting. When you hurt, I hurt. Let's thank God that you're not in any pain." We bowed our heads and prayed. I kissed her several times about the face. Then on the lips. "Go and tell the others how well I'm doing," she repeated.

Eagerly, I obliged her. As I started through the door, I turned around and looked back at Cindy. Just as I did, she raised up on one elbow and grinned her biggest grin and gave me a thumbs up. I returned the thumbs up and noticed she was holding the pink bunny in her hand.

With no forewarning of the nightmare to come, I hurried to share the good news with family and friends who had come to wait with us. I stayed with them for about two minutes. When I started back to Cindy, I saw a telephone just inside the labor and delivery door. I quickly dialed my sister, Ramona, and gave her a sixty-second progress report. Just as I was hanging up the phone, I heard the terrifying emergency code tear into the hospital quietness. I ran toward Cindy's room. Somehow I knew she was in trouble.

Cindy's in trouble. . . Cindy's in trouble. . . . The words tumbled through my mind in our bedroom that long and terrible night. With a burst of fire and thunder, my mind played back the awful scene of Cindy's death. "It's true! It's true!" I jerked myself straight up on the bed. "She's really dead! Oh, God, I can't wake up—I'm already awake! No, no, no! this is not right. This is not fair!"

My golden future had turned to ashes in my hand. A part of forever was missing. The man who had everything suddenly had nothing.

About five o'clock in the morning I drifted into an exhausted sleep. The last sound I heard was the cry of a baby. I didn't know where it came from. There was no baby in my house. Was God telling me that a baby had been born that day? That my baby was just a heartbeat away, in another home? That my baby and Cindy were more alive than ever before, and I would see them. . . one day?

Chapter 5

The Coronation

The light of Thursday's dawn found its way through my bedroom window. I awoke from a brief sleep feeling exhausted and more alone than I'd ever thought possible. Today is the day of Cindy's funeral. I still couldn't believe it. I closely identified with a statement I found later in my files. Robinson said of his mourned wife, "It is not that I am lonely for you. . . . I am mutilated, for you were a part of me."

In a strange kind of trance, I allowed family and close friends Richard Hogue, Jay Strack, Rick Stanley, Ron Long, and others to guide the necessary activities of the day. Although I made major decisions concerning Cindy's funeral service and burial—decisions such as who would officiate, where she would be buried, what clothes she would wear—little questions kept arising. I needed my friends to help me make those decisions and to see that the arrangements were carried out. Their contributions were invaluable in the first days of sadness and in the days that followed.

Cindy's memorial service was planned for eleven o'clock in the morning. I was at the funeral home by nine-thirty greeting people from all walks of Cindy's life. Eventually, the most dreaded of moments arrived. I was to look at Cindy for the last time. Forcing one foot in front of the other, I moved toward the steel-blue casket.

Others thoughtfully left us alone. She was wearing her favorite dress, a printed silk I'd bought for her. Her hands were folded over her Bible.

Unexplainable parting thoughts invaded my mind as reason and emotion did battle with each other. *Why did you leave me, Cindy? You know how I hate to be by myself! Now I have nothing left. . . nothing to live for. . . no reason to go on.*

Cindy and I had treaded some deep waters in our marriage. We had worked through many problems and brought our relationship into the sweetest stage we had ever enjoyed. How impossible it was that I could be standing in a funeral home looking at her lifeless form. The chain that joined my heart to hers tugged again as I studied the physical characteristics of my wife. I knew she was not in the casket that day, but this was the tiny body and the beautiful face that I loved. Hardly a day passed that I was not able to hold her hand, feel her warmth, and catch the scent of her hair. I would miss the physical familiarity of Cindy as much as I would miss her vivid personality and sweet spirit. And in just moments our separation would be complete. It is so hard to say goodbye! No, it's impossible to say goodbye to a part of yourself.

Oh, God, how could you take her? We are so young . . . why now when we had so much promise? I trusted You to look after Cindy and the baby. This is not the way the story was supposed to end!

I doubled my fist as rising anger joined forces with my hopelessness. Moaning and mangled, I began to beat the side of the casket with all the strength I could find. Beating and beating, I slid to the floor crying, "It's not fair! It's not fair! It's not fair!"

On my knees before Cindy's casket that day, I challenged God and called into question everything I'd ever believed about Him. The Father we'd shared let me pour out the frustration, anger, and grief of my broken heart. In looking back, I know that He loved and understood as I battered the casket and railed against Him.

Cindy was carried to New Hope Baptist Church for the funeral. Many people loved her, and hundreds of them crowded into the sanctuary and the television overflow room that had been provided. *How quickly our lives can change!* I thought as I sat in the pew facing the casket that held what was to have been my future. I had planned to stand beside Cindy and dedicate our baby in this sanctuary in just a few weeks. Now I had no wife to stand beside, no baby to give back to God in dedication. In minutes, without warning or premonition, my family was gone.

Richard, Jay, Rick, and Ron officiated. "The crimson of heaven's rainbow is a little brighter today," Ron said, "because Cindy is there." Knowing what a perfectionist Cindy was, Jay commented that he could just see her buzzing around heaven putting things in order. . . probably suggesting that the throne would look better moved just a little to the right. Those who were thinking more clearly than I reminded me of my belief that the best part of a Christian's life begins after death.

I heard the reading of one of Cindy's favorite scriptures, "I am the resurrection and the life. He who believes in Me, though he may die, he shall live. And whoever lives and believes in Me shall never die" (John 11:25-26).

By rote, I prayed: "Father, Cindy was the queen of my life. In a very different sense, today is her coronation day. It's not a day of death at all. Help me to rejoice with her." The best I knew how, I put Cindy to rest in the hands of God.

My ministerial staff served as pallbearers. Following the service, they carried Cindy from the church to the long, white hearse and lifted her in. The heavy door thumped closed with a muffled sound of finality. As a pastor, I frequently stand behind a hearse, I see the casket slide in, and I hear the swooshing thud of the big door. Even today, that sound brings a stab of termination to my heart.

Rodney Schell stood close on one side of me. The dismay and hopelessness carved on his face mirrored my own impassioned sentiment; all that was good and happy in life had been shut away, leaving only gloomy question marks across the future.

Chapter 6
Looking for New Hope

We took Cindy to the little New Hope Cemetery across the street from the church. I wanted her buried among New Hope people. . . people who had had deep meaning in her life. I walked between Rodney and Dr. Harry Smith. Dr. Smith, a fellow minister and friend, was a man in his eighties. I leaned heavily on him feeling his giant-oak sturdiness, knowing his roots were deep and strong. He had seen so much of life, had weathered many storms of pain and loss, and had come through stronger than before. If God had brought him through, He would do it for me too.

As we crossed New Hope Road on that warm, sunny day in March, I could almost see Cindy and myself singing on our way down the same winding road the first time. We had come to the New Hope Church for the Wednesday night prayer service. Pastor Richard Lee had invited me to visit in view of becoming summer youth director. . . an invitation I had every reason to be grateful for. Unemployed for several months, I'd been going to school and working wherever I could find something to do and preaching wherever I was invited. The call to New Hope answered some ponderous prayers for us.

Excitement wouldn't begin to describe what we felt as we drove from Atlanta down Georgia Highway 85 and turned onto New Hope Road. I had lived in the city so long, the rural look of that part of Fayette County refreshed me. We cranked our heads left and right to catch our first glimpse of the church.

"I'll bet that's it!" I exclaimed when I spotted the two buildings that made up New Hope at that time. The greatest cathedral in all Christendom couldn't have looked as magnificent as that new, four-hundred-seat sanctuary and the little, white, pristine church that sat beside it. Deep inside, I knew we had found a home—a happy home where God would use us in His work. A chance to begin again. We had new hope for our lives and for our ministry.

In the sadness of the hour of Cindy's burial, I was grateful for New Hope. Only God could have brought about the circumstances that enabled me to be the church's pastor. I spent a happy two years and two months with Richard Lee as his youth minister and assistant pastor. I shared his vision for New Hope and could see it becoming a reality.

When Richard decided to leave the church and go into full-time evangelism, I was surprised and concerned. I had not imagined New Hope without Richard. In their kindness, the folks of the church wanted to "give the kid a break," so they asked me to become interim pastor while the search committee looked for someone permanent. I furnished them with resumes of other pastors and helped them search in any way that seemed appropriate. Although I knew my job was on the line, I wanted to see them get the right man for New Hope. . . God's appointed man, a man who would dream with them.

The church flourished even under the temporary arrangement. Richard had turned many corners with New Hope, and he had taught me along the way. Even without a permanent pastor, the people endeavored to reach others for Christ. They wanted the church to grow. And grow it did!

During that interim period, I renewed my commitment to the ministry. At an evangelism conference, I heard a minister say that preachers sometimes prostitute a church by using it as a stepping-stone in their own careers. I knew this kind of thing probably happened, but I had not faced the fact that I might be tempted to do that. I saw anew the sacredness of the church. And I covenanted with God that I would make every decision, plan every plan with that sacredness in mind. I vowed to give myself to the work of seeing New Hope, or whatever church I pastored, grow in its commitment to be the church that God wanted it to be.

In one of his sermons, Vance Havner used an illustration that goes something like this: When a preacher stands to preach, the pews before him hold a spouse who has lost a mate, a couple facing possible divorce, a college student who is going through a crisis in faith, a person changing vocations—and a nine-year-old paper doodler who needs Jesus.

In a single message, the minister seeks to meet all these and other diverse needs. The only way it can happen is for the "Wind from Elsewhere" to take his words, give them life, and blow over the audience and into the hearts of the listeners. As the Wind touches, the spouse finds strength to go on without the loved one, the couple learns a new love and stability in Christ, the college student finds the answer to his crisis, the one facing a change of vocation is encouraged and directed— and the nine-year-old paper doodler finds Jesus.

I preached with this philosophy, depending on the Holy Spirit to blow over those to whom I spoke and do the work I could not do. The amazing Wind blessed the church, meeting the needs of the people. We began receiving members by the tens and twenties on a single Sunday. We called those our double-digit days as God did some wonderful things at New Hope.

In the wake of extraordinary growth, I was asked to become the permanent pastor of the church. Deacon Lester Bray, on behalf of the search committee, approached me with the idea, explaining that the church saw no reason to make a change when God was obviously using the present arrangement. What a wonderful church! I could never have started my pastorate with a finer fellowship.

At New Hope we adopted the rainbow as our logo. Along with the logo we often use the words, "As a prism receives the sunlight and spreads its rainbow colors across the earth, so we of the church, receiving the light of God's Spirit, are separated and designated in service. We become His living rainbow, touching the world." New Hope is a rainbow-kind of church, full of joy, full of hope for a better tomorrow.

Cindy fit the environment so well, for she too was filled with joy and hope. The years at New Hope were good ones for Cindy and me. The people cared about us, supported and loved us. They were excited about our baby, letting us know that our baby was the church's baby. Through the years, they shared our laughter and our tears, just as we shared theirs. The day Cindy was buried was a day of shared sorrow. New Hope mourned the loss of a lady who embodied the rainbow spirit of its ministry.

I had never realized how immeasurably I would need the philosophy of my own preaching. I couldn't have known that I would fall into such critical need for the benevolent breath of God, the "Wind from Elsewhere."

Standing at Cindy's graveside, I saw tears on other faces. *These are my people,* I thought. *I've helped them rear their kids. I've married them and buried their loved ones. Hundreds of times I've assured them that God is with us in the nights that have no dawn. Now they are looking at me. Will they see a man able to live by his own testimony. . . or will they see a man destroyed?*

Father, I want them to see Your faithfulness. I'm claiming Your strength. Help me!

Little did I realize that I was embarking on the impossible course of trying to be more than I was for the sake of other people. I so desperately wanted to be the right kind of pastor and the supreme example of the way a Christian should react to the death of a loved one.

In the cemetery, I stood with my hand on the casket for the last time. I spoke brief words to those gathered around and prayed aloud. The burial was completed.

Later I chose a headstone that I felt symbolized the

bond Cindy and I had on this earth, as well as the hope we shared for the future. Made of grey marble, it was designed in the shaped of two hearts and engraved with double wedding rings and orange blossoms. One heart reads:

> Cindy Mitchell Reighard
> And Baby Reighard
> December 3, 1952
> March 1, 1983

And at the bottom:

"We are confident, I say, and willing rather to be absent from the body and to be present with the Lord" (2 Corinthians 5:8).

The second heart holds a blank place for my name. To die and be with Cindy again, I felt, was the most I had to look forward to.

The lines John Bright wrote for his wife who died two short years after their marriage became very precious to me.

> A little while to walk with you, my own—
> Only a little way.
> The one of us must weep and walk alone
> Until God's day.
>
> A little way! It is so sweet to live
> Together, that I know
> Life would not have one withered rose to give,
> If one of us should go.
>
> And if these lips should ever learn to smile
> With thy heart far from mine,
> T'would be for joy that in a little while
> They would be kissed by thine.

Friends and loved ones went their separate ways. Shock began to melt into sadness, and I started my journey on the road of grief. It was a lonely road. In so many ways, life is a singular experience. We are born one-by-one; we come to the Lord one-by-one; and we go out into eternity one-by-one. Our deepest emotional experiences are our own. Though it helps when others bring themselves alongside us, in one very real sense we grieve alone.

If I could have only grasped the truth that God is in everything—performing in my life by His agenda—it would have helped me then. I was a broken man as I turned from Cindy's grave and walked away from New Hope Cemetery. Yet there was no problem with God's calendar; the events of my life were occurring right on schedule.

> There is a time for everything,
> and a season for every activity under heaven:
> a time to be born and a time to die,. . .
> a time to weep and a time to laugh,
> a time to mourn and a time to dance. . .
>   Ecclesiastes 3:1-4 (NIV)

Cindy's time to die had come. The baby's time to die had come too, as impossible as that was to explain. My time to weep, my time to mourn was at hand. Once again I was looking for new hope.

Chapter 7

To Win with Honor

Being at home without Cindy was almost more than I could bear. Coping with time that stood still, especially at home, was one of my most difficult grief tasks. Friends and church folks were faithful to call and come by, but I was running into endless, empty hours. The hands on the Seth Thomas defiantly held their position, and I began to doubt the old adage that "time heals all things." Time seemed to be more enemy than friend. I found that odd, for I'd always been so short of time before the sands in the hourglass became frozen by grief.

My ever-accommodating buddy, Rodney, had accepted my invitation (it was more of a plea. . . . no, more of a command, like one in the section: "Other Duties as Assigned by the Pastor") to live with me during those months of loneliness. One afternoon a few days after Cindy's funeral, time's saddest wings drooped over me. About four-thirty I had a sudden inspiration and said to Rodney, "Man, let's get out of here."

"Where to?" Rodney asked, thinking I probably wanted to go to the cemetery.

"Not the cemetery this time." I guessed his thoughts. "I want you to take me to downtown Atlanta."

"Downtown Atlanta? Right now?" No wonder Rodney was shocked. Nobody hits Atlanta at five o'clock in the afternoon on Friday unless it's absolutely necessary. "I want to go to Five Points in downtown Atlanta," I repeated. "I want to see life at its very busiest."

We reached Five Points in the middle of the afternoon hubbub. Rodney drove slowly around Central City Park and along the streets that create a unique, lacy pattern in the center of Atlanta. I was on my old stomping ground there, for my boyhood home was only minutes from Five Points. As a kid I rode my bike into Atlanta hundreds of times. Looking around me, I thought nostalgically of the days when we lived in the inner city. For years I slugged my way up in one of the country's roughest neighborhoods.

It struck me that day that fighting was something I'd always done. Sure, fighting depression and hopelessness was a new kind of conflict, but I knew how to fight. I grew up in a wild and crazy place, one where fighting was practically a requirement for survival. In an attempt to avoid the label of "sissy," I bent a few rules and broke a few laws. And I learned to use my fists. All the boys of Howell Station fought. We fought to protect ourselves, and we fought for recreation.

A rough and rugged crowd called the Howell Station neighborhood home. It was a community in transition. It consisted of a mill village, a Black ghetto, and a low-income white section. Generally, the community people felt a kind of friendliness for each other—maybe more of a belonging. We didn't ask questions about each other's business. Usually, we didn't want to know it. The adults went their way, and the kids did their thing too. Although I never became one of the hardest breed, I saw daily what might be termed the low-life of an inner city. I struggled to stay in the middle of the road, wanting to be tough but not wanting to become as crude or cruel as those who ruled that neck of the woods. For twenty-seven years my environment included profuse profanity, vulgarity, drunkenness, child abuse, wife beating, disregard for every moral law. In my own way, I fought to be a balanced person. I didn't want to stay in Howell Station forever.

As Rodney and I sat in the car at Five Points looking up and down those Atlanta streets, I saw a collage of humanity. People crisscrossed in every direction as they hurried to their next appointment. Some laughed and talked, but others bore serious faces. Masses gathered at the bus stops and pushed to get aboard. Businessmen carried attache' cases. Couples held hands. Teenagers with boomboxes shucked and jived. A child fell on the sidewalk. An old man walked with a cane.

Those people don't even know that Cindy's dead, I thought. *For them it's business as usual. . . just like any other day. The world is staying right on schedule and all of life is moving on. How can it be? It doesn't seem right.* I felt like crying out, "Hey folks, don't you know my wife died? Isn't it written all over my face? My world has crashed, and you don't even care!"

I tried to turn from that kind of reaction to something constructive. And being in that setting proved to be extremely therapeutic. Remembering my past struggles and watching the busy life at Five Points, I was able to turn a corner in the way I felt about my lonely future. In that setting, God gave me a crystal clear message:

> Ike, all of this life you see around you isn't going to stop. It's up to you to decide how much time you will take out of your life before you pick yourself up and go on. You can take a month, three months, six. . . a year. Or you can take a lifetime. What will it be?

I knew in that rendezvous at Five Points, the Lord wanted me to begin to put things back together the best way I knew how. I was a fighter and I determined to do what it took to make the best of what was left of my life. "I will win," I promised God. "And You will be honored." Then, in my humanness, I added to my vow: "And Cindy, you will be proud of me. I'll work harder, I'll live better, I'll do it for three people—not just one. I wonder if I've ever been fully spiritual!"

At this point I could write in the role of "The Super Christian" and say that I gave it all to God that day, that He took away the pain, and things were easy from then on. But that would be a lie. Incredible suffering followed, and the greatest battle of my life, though invisible to others, waged for many months.

The difference was that I had taken up the gauntlet with a new strength and determination. I had grasped the tip of the truth that victory was up ahead. I knew that somehow I would be a part of the mainstream of life once again because that was my choice. And, after all, God had mentioned something about "everlasting arms underneath."

Chapter 8

Currents and Crosscurrents

As grief took its full toll, my robust imagination double-timed to produce a network of emotional currents and crosscurrents. I hotly debated all of the whys of life and death in a way I'd never done before. I don't believe for a moment that it is unspiritual for a Christian to ask "Why?" in experiences of heartbreak. I believe it is natural and honest. If I ever doubted that, I changed my mind when my time came. More than once I heard the cry of my own voice: "Why?"

Although I have seen positive things come out of the death of Cindy and the baby, I've never really settled in my mind and heart why they died. Cindy loved and trusted God. The why questions that bombarded me at the time of Cindy's funeral persisted as I went about the business of trying to live without her. Why would He cut her life short? Why would He give us the baby and then take them both? It seemed downright stupid.

Cindy had given purpose to my life. It was through her that I became a Christian in the first place. I had always told Cindy that I was a Christian because she would have never dated me, let alone married me, if she had known that I didn't know the Lord. I had confused being a Christian with simply believing there is a God and being born in America. I was so clueless—if I'd been born in a garage I would have thought I was a Ford!

Although I knew some of the language and had a reasonable grasp of Christian behavior, I was not a Christian.

But in the fall of 1973, something happened that changed all that. Cindy and I went with the Reverend John Yarbrough and our youth group to Rockridge Baptist Assembly for a retreat. I was to be in charge of the recreational activities. After we got on the bus—too late to back out—John told me he wanted me to help with some of the teaching. He gave me the topic: "The Role of the Holy Spirit in Our Lives." How clever of John! He knew I would have to give that subject a lot of soul-searching thought.

It was "fake it till you make it" for me all through that first day as I tried to work with the young people and struggle with the role of the Holy Spirit in my own life. In the evening, after the kids were as settled as kids at camp ever are, I went outside to be alone for a few minutes. Distant lights and a nearly full moon lit the path I followed up a little hill. Reaching the top, I stopped and leaned against a big pine tree. The sweet evergreen scent in the air, the beauty and peace all around me, and a growing conviction in my heart brought me very close to God. Thinking of all that had been said that day, I made a long overdue admission to myself: *Here I am masquerading as a Christian, trying to teach boys and girls about Christ, and I don't even know what I'm talking about.* I wanted more than anything else in the world to receive Jesus as my Savior and to let Him live His life through me. I decided to tell Him so: "God, You know what I'm feeling. I believe that You love me and sent Your Son to die for me. I accept Him now as my personal Lord and Savior." I didn't see any angels, hear a choir, or see a vision. But I made a commitment for which I have always been grateful, especially during the dark times. Without Christ in my heart, I don't believe I would have made it through the "valley of the shadow of death."

John joined me shortly. I explained what was going on with me, although I was sure he already knew. In minutes I saw Cindy coming up the hill to find me. One of the greatest joys of my life was telling Cindy that I was one with her in Christ, and this time it was for real. John prayed aloud and the three of us shared the most sacred experience any person can claim: my birth into the eternal kingdom of God.

I knew from the time of that commitment God would lead me into a Christian vocation. The evening I accepted Jesus Christ, I also heard Him ask, "Do you, Ike Reighard, accept My assignment for you, whatever it might be?" And for the second time in my life I vowed, "I do," committing all that I was or ever hoped to be.

Cindy's spiritual strength had been so important to me. Why was it taken away? Over and over I asked myself if I thought God took Cindy to punish me for something. I finally concluded that couldn't be the case— God didn't have to go through Cindy or the baby to get to me. He could have dealt with me directly. I could have been taken or strickened. That was not the answer.

Well, I continued to challenge, *maybe God is out of control. Maybe evil has triumphed in this world after all.* That frightening prospect was a real consideration for me as my sorrow battered me back and forth. I was struck with a terrible tragedy, and to make it worse there was no explanation for it.

Since I couldn't answer "why?", I turned to asking "why now?" Why did God let Cindy and me go through a time of strain in our marriage, then when life came to such a perfect time, take Cindy in death? Why did He begin so much with us and then end it? And yet, in facing "why now?", I had to consider the question, "When would have been a good time for Cindy to die? After the baby was born? When the baby was four years old?. . . or ten? After forty years of marriage?. . . or fifty?" There would never have been a right time for Cindy to leave me.

The next question, of course, was "why me?" or "why us?" I knew early on, though, that to entertain that viewpoint would infer that it was okay for someone else to suffer—as long as it didn't touch me. As a Christian, I had to surrender that one too.

After wrestling long and hard with the "why" questions, I finally realized I was losing the battle. The only way I could win was to give it up altogether. I didn't want to be a slave to questions that have no answers. C.S. Lewis, in *A Grief Observed,* said as he mourned for his wife: "When I lay these questions before God I get no answer, but a rather special sort of 'no answer.' It is not the locked door. It is more like a silent, certainly not uncompassionate, gaze. As though He shook His head not in refusal but waiving the question. Like, 'Peace, child; you don't understand.'"[1] I came to see that the thing to do was to leave my dead-end questions with God. Yes, I would have to work on that.

With waning emotional strength, I regrouped for the fight and reached for my most brutal weapon—anger. My anger produced some behavior that was strange even to me. I did and said some things that were unacceptable from any adult, much less a minister. Something finally happened that brought this into focus for me. Rodney and I took a trip to Florida for a few days of rest. While lounging by the pool one day, I was joined by a lady who wanted to be friendly. "Well, what brings you to Florida?" she asked. Feeling anything but friendly and intending to share my misery, I snarled back at her, "My wife died." The lady's expression confirmed that I'd set her completely adrift. I didn't even care.

On the same trip, I was strolling along the beach one morning, watching the sea gulls, shelling. . . just trying to relieve my ever-present tension. I came across an older man who looked as sad as I felt. In a little better mood than previously, I spoke to the stranger and casually asked him what kind of morning he was having. "Not so good," he answered. "But you wouldn't understand."

"Give me a try, my friend." My pastoral spirit returned for a moment. "You might be surprised." Sadly, he told me why he was so downcast, "I just buried my wife." A strange coincidence? I doubt it. These two events brought sharply to my realization that people needed my concern, not my bitterness, and I was not improving my lot by making other people unhappy.

Desperately lonely, I had become a stranger to myself. Pain and confusion kept swelling inside of me. I wondered how I would contain it and still go on as a decent, caring human being. Whatever would become of me?

Chapter 9
Robin

Edmund Burke said, "Next to love, sympathy is the divinest passion of the human heart." I needed someone who really knew how I felt. I needed someone near my age who knew what it was to lose the one you had planned to spend your life with. . . someone who knew what it felt like to have your dreams smashed. God had a unique answer for that need.

Several months before Cindy died, a young lady by the name of Robin Covington joined New Hope Baptist Church. Robin had come to know Christ under the guidance of one of our ministers, and when she came forward in the church to confess Him publicly, I introduced her to our congregation with smiles and cheer. "Many of you know Robin. She lost her fiance' a few months ago in a tractor accident. And now God is going to put her life back together and give her a wonderful future."

It was easy then, in my ignorance, to think how one can make a simple effort and put a life back together. I learned better, though. Once you've been there, it's no longer quite so easy.

When I baptized Robin, I remember thinking, *This lady sure needs to smile. She has the most expressionless face and the blankest eyes I've ever seen.* She was breathing and existing, but I couldn't see a spark of life in her.

Later when I looked into the mirror and saw that my face was void of expression and my eyes were blank, I recognized the lifeless existence I'd seen in Robin Covington.

Robin didn't come to see me when Cindy died, but she sent word that she would be glad to talk with me if I thought she could be of help. Actually, she had not impressed me as being one I'd like to talk to ordinarily because of her apparent lack of joy. I didn't know how she was getting along at that point. But she had offered to help, and maybe her experience would be similar to mine. Maybe she would understand. . . maybe she would even have some answers.

My decision to ask her to talk with me came about one evening as I flew in from an out-of-state speaking engagement. When the pilot announced our approach to the Atlanta Airport, I buckled my seatbelt and prepared for the landing. Taxing to the gate, I thought of how Cindy used to come pick me up when I returned from a trip. She always parked the car and came to the gate to meet me, making each homecoming a happy occasion. As soon as I entered the terminal, I would look around for her, and there she'd be with outstretched arms and that wonderful smile just for me. What a welcome!

The familiar heaviness filled my chest that night as I thought of the crowd at the gate. . . without Cindy. Others from the plane would be welcomed with warmth and kisses, but not me. When I entered the terminal, I was glad to see that Wesley Bethea, one of our ministers, and his date had come to meet me. His date was Susan Covington, Robin's sister. As we walked up the concourse together, I put my arm around Susan and said, "I wish you would tell your sister I want to talk to her sometime. She's the only person I know, near my age, who has gone through what I have."

Soon after that on a Wednesday night following prayer service, Robin came to the front of the church and spoke to me. "I understand you'd like to talk to me."

"Yes, I would. If you don't mind," I responded.

Robin looked serious. "If you are interested in talking about what you're going through, I'll be glad to see if I can help." We agreed that I'd call her later, and we would get together.

At that time, there were four single ministers on our staff. We had joined the Marriott Health Club to swim, play tennis, work out, or just get away when we felt the need. One night Rodney, Wes, and I decided to go for a swim. They both had dates, and since Wes' date was Susan Covington, we invited Robin to join us too.

After a good swim, Robin got out and sat down at a table along the poolside. I talked with her casually from the water for a while and then got out and pulled up a chair by the table. It was the first time I'd ever had a conversation of any depth with Robin. I had a burning need to ask her about her own experience and share my hurts with her, even though I felt awkward and vulnerable about doing it. After all, I was her pastor. I was supposed to be the one with the answers. And besides that, I wasn't sure she really knew hurt as deep and complete as mine. I guess it's easy to think, *My pain is greater than your pain.* I wondered if she would understand after all.

I was pleasantly surprised, however, when I immediately found Robin easy to talk to. Not wanting to pour out her suffering to me, she was slow to tell me what she had been through. Her only concern, it seemed, was to help me unload my burden and deal with my own loss . . . my own doubts and fears.

I began to see Robin in a new light. I think I really looked at her for the first time. She had changed. Man, had she changed! She'd thrown off the shackles of sadness that restricted her natural glow. Even her body spoke a different language. She moved with surety—an athletic flair combined with grace and femininity. Thick, chestnut brown hair hung down her back, sweeping her skin which was bronzed by the summer sun. The expressionless face I remembered now smiled at me with tenderness and a hint of the peace I was searching for. Eyes that had been vacant now looked at me with warmth and compassion beneath the longest lashes I'd ever seen.

As Robin and I talked, we both sensed an immediate kinship. I felt that I'd known her all my life. When I cried,

I knew she didn't think less of me as a man. She understood by pain, and it seemed to hurt her too. I once heard empathy defined as "your pain in my heart." In that sense, Robin was a true empathizer. Her entrance into my life was the dawn of new healing for me.

And the best was yet to be.

Chapter 10
A Downward Spiral

During that first conversation with Robin at the Marriott Club, I had the strangest feeling she would become an important part of my life. I wanted her to be a part of my life. It shocked me when I suddenly thought of her as a wife. *Oh, God, how can I think like this while I'm still aching for Cindy—how could there possibly be room in my heart for anyone else?*

I wanted to see Robin again. I needed to see her. But wanting to be with her at that point seemed wrong. Confused about my jumbled feelings, I began to weave myself into an emotional web. My network of devastation included grief from the loss of Cindy and the baby, guilt over not being a perfect husband, inordinate anxiety, and depression that negated any hope of a future. And now to compound it all, I felt guilty for having involuntary romantic thoughts about Robin. My downward spiral accelerated, in spite of all I could do.

The sun rose, the sun set. I threw myself into my work, but I found no relief from my chaotic emotions. I couldn't have made it in those days without Rodney. He had been one of Cindy's best friends. It was as if she had invested the love of friendship in him so he could return it to me when she was gone. He stuck by me. . . close by. Poor guy, he even slept in the room with me because I had such a hard time making it through the nights. I don't know how he ever got any sleep since all night, every night, I kept the television and lights on.

Eugenia Price's words in *Getting Through the Night* are incredibly accurate: "Nights have always come as regularly as days. In a sense, they should not be unfamiliar to us but when the familiar, harmonious patterns of our life have just been shredded, nights can be the very worst times of all. When a beloved one is suddenly gone—nights seem to make the loss unbearable. . . The aching heart can somehow survive peopled, light-filled days. Darkness has long been the symbol of loneliness, of being lost; the symbol of danger, of dread, of weeping."[1]

Lying in my bed, night after night, I fought a parade of ugly visions when I closed my eyes. I was afraid to face the truth that Cindy would never come back—then I'd have the strangest fear that I'd imagined it all and that she would come back. "Oh, God, keep her dead, cause if You don't, I'll know I've lost my mind!" Nightmares screamed within me when I dozed. Then with a pounding heart and body wet with perspiration, I'd burst into terrified consciousness.

Night after night I fought the waves of panic and desolation that lapped over me.

All kinds of ideas about my own death threatened me: *You know you're going to be next, don't you? Keep a vigil—you never know when or how.* Every time I heard of a plane crash or some other tragedy, every time I saw a person in a wheelchair or heard of a terminal illness, I immediately identified! Maybe my mission has ended too. My ambivalent prayer became, "Oh, God, I've got to get out of this—I want to die! Oh, God, don't let me die!"

I slept maybe three hours a night, and that was not a restful sleep. The doctor offered me a sleep medication, but I refused it. Taking medicine would only confirm that I wasn't strong enough to get through it by myself.

Although the days offered opportunities to keep my mind diverted, they were not much better than the night. I couldn't make myself eat meals at home. Cindy's empty place at our table was just too specific a reminder. Eating out all the time got old, so ultimately my nutrition suffered.

Then there were the pity parties. "It's my party and I'll cry if I want to." *Why should I have to endure this kind of pain?* I thought. *Look at all those murderers and thieves out there—they deserve this. I don't. Nobody else ever hurt like I do, and I want everybody to stop what they're doing and hurt with me. Isn't anybody listening? Doesn't anybody care?*

The reproach of my conscience was probably the greatest burden of all. Challenging my own faith, I heard the constant accusation: *Why do you think Cindy really died? Do you think you could pray and raise her up? You know you wouldn't have to suffer like this if you'd pray the prayer of faith. It's all you fault anyway. If you'd been the man God called you to be, it wouldn't have been necessary for Him to take Cindy. We get what we deserve in this life, you know. It's one big slot machine. Put in good behavior, pull the lever, and watch your dreams come true.* Since the lever had brought up tragedy, I must have put in some kind of incorrect behavior. And now I faced the issue of what I should do about Robin.

Unable to concentrate, I found it difficult to study. Everything I did was difficult, yet doing nothing was the most difficult thing of all. The need to stay occupied flung me into all kinds of busywork. Never before had I noticed that all my dresser drawers needed straightening. I organized my underwear and did the same for my socks. Frantically compelled to do little things about the house and office that had never interested me before, I straightened and fixed, and then planned what I'd work on next. It was all a part of my fight to stay afloat. With no sense of joy, I found that the mornings introduced days that were becoming as hard as the nights.

In the midst of all this, I was desperately trying to be a good pastor. I knew others in my congregation were dealing with loss, just as I was. They were down, and the last thing they needed to see was their pastor falling apart. More than anything, I wanted to show them that God helps us through our sorrow. Despite all my efforts to be strong, at times I sat at my desk and cried like a baby. I sincerely began to doubt that God was ever going to help me.

Trying to keep my suffering to myself and appear to have more endurance than I had became a heavy load to carry. It eventually locked me in a deadly hold from which I could not free myself. It humiliated me to admit that I was scared—I was a grown man, a minister of the gospel!—but it was true. I was scared to death! Depleted physically from the strain, I developed heart palpitations. And, of course, that increased my fear. Frequent trips to the doctor didn't help much. Afraid to die and afraid not to, my anxiety and depression were getting out of control. *Just hang on until five o'clock. Just hang on till the weekend. Just hang on till vacation. Just hang on till morning. It's bullet time! Just hang on! Just hang on! Just hang on! Time will heal this. . . but God, time is not moving!* Bereft of confidence and hope, I quit trying to win and just tried not to lose.

An invisible wall separated me from the rest of the world. I felt strange and displaced. Looking in the mirror during one of my most awful moments, I felt as if I were outside myself, looking at the reflection of someone else. Sad and hollow-eyed, writhing and struggling, I wept and cried aloud, "Won't somebody help that man!" New fear enshrouded me when I realized "that man" was me. I had to get a grip on myself, but I didn't know how.

Chapter 11
The Ladder of Recovery

Relief from grief never comes overnight no matter what the spiritual condition of the one who grieves, and I'm not about to claim that it does. Recovery is like a ladder we climb one rung at a time. I knew my answers were to be found in God. I had dutifully observed all the "victorious living" principles as I understood them. I knew somehow God was going to take care of me, but the wounds of bereavement remained open and hurting as I searched for the way in which He would bring healing.

I received advice from all directions. Christians wanted to be sure I really knew what the Spirit-filled life was all about. "Hang in there and pray," was the advice I got most often. I did my best at that, but eventually I discovered that while hanging and praying made for an impressive spiritual testimony, it was not the total solution to my dilemma. "That man" needed some insight, some support from someone trained to counsel and encourage. Finally giving in to the facts, I decided to see a professional counselor.

Several years earlier at New Hope, we had contracted with Christian Counseling Service, Inc., to provide for the counseling needs of our congregation and others who came to us. It had long been my philosophy that the church should try to meet the mental and emotional needs of people just as we try to meet their spiritual and physical needs. We cannot always "work through" our difficulties alone. It seems to me that the scripture verse, "in the multitude of counselors there is safety" (Proverbs 11:14), encourages us to go outside ourselves for new perspectives. Christian psychological counseling by well-qualified professionals can save our lives.

Dr. Ron Braund, director of this ministry, and his staff were helping many people with emotional difficulties. God was working through them as they dealt compassionately with their clients. Ron had occasionally spent time with me as a friend since Cindy's death. He had served as my counselor when I asked questions of him. But the time had come when I needed to make a point of seeing him on a regular, professional basis and discover why I continued to dig my emotional rut deeper and darker. I benefited enormously from the counsel of this good man.

Our meetings were not necessarily structured. Sometimes we went to McDonalds, sometimes Ron came to my office, and sometimes I went to his. I didn't mind being seen there. They tell me the ratio of people who can be helped by a good counselor is one out of one. I figured I fit into that ratio somewhere. Objective and unbiased, Ron let me say anything I wanted to say in any way I chose to say it. I could vent my anger, frustration, fears, and tears. He'd seen it all before. I could be myself no matter how negative a self that was, and I was still okay to him. I couldn't shock him. He never passed judgment. Ron asked me questions I didn't know how to ask myself. He touched on feelings I had not defined and dealt with.

Perhaps the first helpful principle I learned was that I needed to understand my "point of view." Each of us sees and reacts to life from his or her own point of view. A person's point of view is determined by genetic, environmental, and situational circumstances. In other words, "our viewing point" determines our point of view. And it is often more important to understand our viewing point than our point of view. If we find ourselves thinking and reasoning in a circle—or a rut—we usually need to move from where we are to a different vantage point. And sometimes we can't do this alone. We need someone to help us.

I was interpreting a number of issues in an unhealthy way. Ron helped me to understand why I thought the way I did, and he led me to a more healthy viewing place. This new perspective resulted in fresh insight and the ability to act on them. To assist me with this, Ron identified a "Needs and Values Concept" that affects every person involved in conflict. This theory embodies the truth that each of us has a set of values (beliefs) and a set of needs (desires). In order to make an emotional recovery, it was necessary for me to distinguish my needs from my values, and examine both in an honest light.

My values came from my belief about the mandates from God, family, peers, and culture. These values included: following the will of God, being a respectable pastor, being strong on family, as well as being loyal to Cindy and those who loved her, and waiting a year before entering a relationship with any other woman. My values were, in a word, those things that I considered right and appropriate.

My needs, on the other hand, were: to be with someone who cared about me, to have a happy life, to do some things that were fun, and to share affection with Robin.

Since I believed some of my feelings (or needs) were inappropriate, I attempted to disregard them or to live above them. I didn't realize that the unmet needs were a valid consideration. When I sought to stand by my values, my needs were repressed. When I tried to get my needs met, I created a values conflict. Failing to "get it right," I moved from self-respect to self-contempt, then to depression and emotional burnout. Without clarification, self-destruction could have been the ultimate outcome.

Losing the battle at both stations in the needs/values struggle, I worried about my role as pastor. I wondered what those under my leadership would think if they really knew me. I couldn't possibly ask them, but I also wondered how those in a similar turmoil were making it through their dark hours. With Ron's guidance, I saw that the answer was within me and not from others. I must reach into myself and use my God-given resources to solve the problem. I must accept my limitations and give up the pretense of being more than I was. It was also necessary for me to make a conscious choice to face my needs and fill them, trusting God to guide me.

In the spiritual realm, I learned that I could receive the joy of the Lord and get on with my life whenever I chose to do so. As Ron said, "If you make the choice, God will make the change." If I launched out on faith in Him, He would prove trustworthy.

I began to make a distinction between sound, God-given values and those I'd picked up in my culture, particularly as they concerned Cindy. My vow to her had been "till death do us part." Now death had parted us— the relationship ended with her death. The sense of missing her would go on and the memories would always be precious, but Cindy was no longer here for me to love. And she and I knew together that human love has its limitations. Although it might have appeared extremely romantic for me to grieve myself to death or throw myself across Cindy's grave in one final gesture of despair, that was not God's way. If I were to be God's man, I had to open up to the healing and happiness He wanted to give me, without waiting on some self-imposed timetable. He wanted to "fix me" just as soon as I was ready.

As I became more enlightened, it occurred to me to wonder why I was arguing with the way God was choosing to meet my needs. Would I be presumptuous enough to think that the Creator of everything could not be creative in the way He cared for me in the most difficult time of my life? I was ready now for Romans 8:28: "We know that in all things God works for the good of those who love him" (NIV). I could finally praise Him as I called that verse to mind, along with the wonderful consolation of Philippians 4:19: "And my God shall supply all your need according to His riches in glory by Christ Jesus." There was no qualification there, no conditions, just a simple promise waiting to be claimed.

I learned something about God that I'd never had occasion to need so desperately before: He was pulling for me. He wanted me to move from the weeping of the night to the joy of the morning. He wanted to give me "beauty for ashes." And I determined to accept with gratitude the healing that God offered, in whatever way He wanted to give it.

Also, in our counseling sessions, Ron and I reviewed the "why" questions I had learned to leave unanswered. He taught me to go from "why?" to "what?" "What are You doing, God? What can I take away from this experience that will benefit me and others? What in this situation will ultimately bring glory to You?" Ron led me from a negative approach to a positive one, from a posture of resignation to my circumstances, to one of using those circumstances to rebuild my life and become a more useful, better-prepared servant of God.

As my insights grew, I could see that the ladder of recovery was a ladder of growth. The maturing life was one in which I achieved new and different perspectives. Each rung was a step in maturity. The final and perfect perspective is at the top with God. I would not reach the top in this life, but the closer I got to Him, the higher and better would be my viewing point. Certainly I would not overcome all my perplexities in this world. Still, I learned in a new way to appreciate the words of Jesus to Paul, "My grace is sufficient for you, for My strength is made perfect in weakness." And Paul's own testimony, "Therefore most gladly I will rather boast in my infirmities, that the power of Christ may rest upon me. Therefore I take pleasure in infirmities, in reproaches, in needs, in persecutions, in distresses, for Christ's sake. For when I am weak, then I am strong" (2 Corinthians 12:9-10).

I climbed yet another rung in my recovery ladder one day when Ralph Cooper came by to see me. Ralph later became one of the ministers at New Hope, but at that time I barely knew him. He had lost his wife by death a few years earlier and was certainly in a position to say, "I know what you are feeling." Ralph had heard me say of Cindy's leaving me, "I'll never get over it."

"You're right, Ike, you never will get over it. Your life has been altered, and what you have gone through will always be a part of you." Hearing from a fellow-traveler—a man my age—a man who had found love and happiness again, was a gift from God. Ralph helped me understand that it was okay for me to feel as if I would never get over my loss. My life was changed and I would always bear the effects of my sorrow. That's the way it was supposed to be, but the alteration didn't have to be a negative force.

Oliver Wendell Holmes once said, "The great thing in the world is not so much where we stand as in what direction we are moving." With new insights and a new outlook, I was moving in the right direction. I was climbing that ladder. I hadn't gone as high as I wanted to go. I hadn't gone as high as I would eventually go, but praise God, I was on my way!

Chapter 12

Reasons of the Heart

With new insights and a new outlook, I came to a better understanding of my grief and my reactions to what I was feeling. I arrived at a healthier "viewing place" where I felt free to develop a relationship with Robin. Blaise Pascal described my situation with his words: "The heart has its reasons which reason knows nothing of." Though my intellectual reasoning may have appeared absent or confused, my heart knew that I needed Robin. I needed her to walk with me as I trudged the bittersweet trail of returning to normal after great trauma.

One of the beautiful mysteries of God is what happens between a man and a woman in love.

> There are three things which are too wonderful
> for me,
> Four which I do not understand:
> The way of an eagle in the sky,
> The way of a serpent on a rock,
> The way of a ship in the middle of the sea,
> And the way of a man with a maid.
> Proverbs 30:18-19 (NASB)

Cindy was the only girl I'd ever been in love with. When she died, I didn't believe I would love anyone else, certainly not for a long time. Yet my relationship with

Robin was growing increasingly important to me. It was not a lusty experience. Robin's strength and compassion attracted me to her. I deeply appreciated her. Although she grew more beautiful to me every time I saw her, her charm had more to do with her supportive and caring spirit than the way she looked. She had lost the most important person in her life too, and she shared her heart with me.

Our first dates, if they could be called that, were meals with other couples. There was always somebody else around. Later, when just the two of us began having dinner together, we sat in restaurants for hours talking about how to put a bruised and battered life back together again. We had so many serious things to talk about that movies or any other form of entertainment seemed a waste of time. I asked her all kinds of questions so I could compare what I was going through with what she had experienced. As a minister I had counseled many people who had lost loved ones. Now Robin was helping me better understand some of my own counseling precepts.

We spent so much quality time sharing and praying together, it didn't take us long to develop a close relationship. I was riveted to Robin by gratitude, affection, agape. . . and eros. One night following dinner and one of our "sessions," I drove Robin home and we sat in the car continuing our discussion. Being near her was wonderful. Looking into her attentive eyes I was moved again by their softness, their warmth. I pressed toward her, put my arms around her, and drew her close. We held each other for an irresistible moment, then gently but passionately we kissed. It sealed the miracle we both held in our hearts. We were in love.

It would seem that finding the freedom to love, and being loved in return, would have quickly ushered in my "happily ever after." But such as not altogether the case. Human nature is peculiar, and my peace of mind was still not totally restored. Because of that, I put up roadblocks at times to the fulfillment of our joy. *It's too good to be true,* I told myself. *Robin can't be from God— she's too wonderful too soon.* I had thought that if mourning for Cindy ever did end, I would have to go through a period of dating and shopping. It had never occurred to me that another "one and only" could be sent from heaven quickly and without my striving.

I even began to entertain the idea that maybe I'd misinterpreted things and Robin was not a gift from God after all. Later Robin teased me and said I accused her of being a witch with a forked tongue and crackling flames of fire leaping from her mouth, and that I prayed over her to exorcise any evil spirits that might be lurking there. I did interrogate her in every way I could think of. "Tell me with your own lips that you know Jesus Christ as your personal Lord and Savior," I commanded. "I want to hear you say it: 'I've been washed by the blood of Christ.'" I figured if she were from the devil, she couldn't handle that.

But Robin cooperated amazingly well and passed every test I threw at her. She thought I was weird, but she answered my questions and said what I needed to hear. Her attitude was, "Well, the guy's been through a lot. I guess I have to excuse some strange behavior."

About the time I finally reconciled the Satan issue, another question arose. One night while we were listening to the radio, a short subject about John F. Kennedy came on. "Where were you when Kennedy was killed?" I asked what I thought was an ordinary question. "Where was I when Kennedy was killed?" she repeated as if she'd never thought about it before. "When was he killed?"

"Don't you know? November 1963." I was ticked. Everybody was supposed to know when Kennedy was killed.

"In my crib, I guess," Robin came back. "I wasn't even two years old."

In her crib!? Surely she's wrong! I was in high school when Kennedy was killed! I felt sick.

"When did you graduate from high school?" I dreaded her answer.

"In 1980," she insisted.

I shot up a quick prayer, *Oh, God, just let her be so dumb that she flunked several grades!* I can't have fallen for a girl that much younger than I am. But careful counting told me what I didn't want to know—Robin was twelve years my junior. How could I have been so mistaken about Robin's age? I thought since she had dated Phil Gray for six years and seemed so mature, she must be at least in her mid-twenties. I had not dreamed that she started dating Phil when she was only fourteen.

In the days that followed, I decided that twelve years was too much age difference between a husband and wife. Since I was already in love, this posed a real problem. While I was still grappling with this age dilemma, I made a trip to Ohio to fill a speaking engagement. Alone there in my hotel room one night, I was reading the biography of my favorite preacher, Peter Marshall. I considered Peter Marshall's sermons, with their graphic illustrations, to be the best I ever studied. I even tried to style my own sermons after his. And I thought Peter and Catherine Marshall had a fabulous relationship. As I was reading that night about their courtship and marriage, I learned that he was exactly twelve years older than she. Through this godly man, whom I had respected so long, the Lord sent me a message: "You see, it's just fine. The minister you've admired the most was successful in a marriage with a woman exactly twelve years younger than he."

I grabbed the phone and called Robin. "Guess what! It's all right for me to be twelve years older than you!"

"I'm glad you got it settled." She said in her inimitable style. "I never considered it a problem."

Though things were falling into place, I continued to examine my heart with regard to my love relationship with Robin. More than anything else I wanted to be in God's will. And I sought the Holy Spirit's guidance as deliberately as I ever had before. I felt unusually close to the Lord as I counted on Him, praying fervently that I would not make a mistake with Robin.

Also, I was determined not to bypass what God wanted to teach me in grief. I had so counted on Cindy and the baby to complete my life. After losing them both, I didn't want to miss anything God had for me in that experience. With all my heart I wanted to pass through every tributary of grief's river that God intended for me to travel and to come forth the man He wanted me to be.

As I prayerfully contemplated remarriage, I remembered an incident that took on new significance. One day, a few months before Cindy died, I inadvertently rubbed my hand across the outside of my throat and discovered an enlarged gland. Knowing that it had not been there before, I reported it to my doctor. He recommended immediate surgery. Prior to the surgery, my family doctor and the surgeon agreed that the most likely diagnosis was Hodgkin's disease.

Staggered by such a grim prospect, Cindy and I discussed some serious issues we had never talked about before. She was pregnant then, and I assured her that if anything happened to me, I thought she should marry again just as quickly as God showed her the right person. I wanted her and the baby to have someone to love them and take care of them. In that discussion, we talked about how much both of us liked being married. . . we were just "old married people." And Cindy expressed the fact that she would not want me to remain single long if anything should happen to her. When my diagnosis turned out to be ossified muscle and nothing to worry about, I put the matter of remarriage out of my mind. Since I was the one facing illness, I was thinking more of Cindy's marrying again. I never thought it would be the other way around. In Eugenia Price's book, *Getting Through the Night*, I found something that satisfied the last thread of my frazzled question, "Am I dishonoring Cindy by loving Robin?" In this inspired work, Miss Price poses the question: "When I lose a loved one, am I wronging that one if I beg God for some answer that will help my pain now?"

"No," she concludes. And in her sensitive wisdom she advances the idea that the beloved one who has gone to be with God sees, without sadness, the needs of those of us who are left behind, and without competition, pulls for us to have those needs met.[1]

Influenced by this interpretation, I could see a smiling Cindy in the "great cloud of witnesses" cheering me on. . . wanting me to have abundant life for what time I have left on earth. God has given her the ability to see and love as He does. She does not see Robin as her rival, but rather as a fellow believer whom God has provided to help make for abundance in my life. No longer bound by time and human limitations, she knows everything is going to turn out right. And in the twinkling of an eye we will all be together in the perfection of the Father's holy love.

In the beauty of this concept, I completely accepted the affirmation that I was free to plan my future with Robin, looking to God for direction. I became convinced that Robin was from the Lord and that it was okay for me to love her and to marry her.

Chapter 13
A New Tomorrow

I was grateful for the assurance that Robin was a gift from God. He wanted me to be happy with her. The only difficulty that remained for me was my concern that some people I cared about might not understand how I could love someone else so soon after Cindy's death. I didn't want to hurt anybody.

When I took Robin out we usually went to places where we thought nobody we knew would see us. Ron Braund helped us by candidly pointing out that to continue in such behavior would be hypocritical. "Let your relationship come naturally to the light," he advised. Robin and I knew we were not doing anything wrong. We didn't have anything to hide. I agreed with Ron, and the first thing I wanted to do was get the opinion of my staff. Once again I applied my verse, "In an abundance of counselors there is victory."

God has always given me wonderful men to work with at New Hope. The staff I went to at that time included Rodney Schell, Wes Bethea, John Jenkins, Roger Christian, Keith Moore, Ron Braund, Carl Mowell, Sr., and Harry Smith. These great men of God were committed to him and His assignment for them at New Hope, and not one of them was afraid to tell me what he thought. I have often likened our staff to the giant sequoia forest. Individual sequoia trees have unimpressive roots, but they cluster together and entwine their roots, giving them the dependent power to grow into huge, magnificent trees. Our staff bonded as brothers, giving strength and finding it in each other, both in personal matters as well as in matters of the church.

It was in that kind of a staff setting that I explained my relationship with Robin. "This is the way it is," I told them. "I've found someone I want to be with. . . one person who meets my needs and brings me happiness. What do you think?" Without exception they encouraged me, "We believe God sent her."

They understood like nobody else the difficulties that confronted me as a single minister. They knew me, and they knew I would be better off married and focused on a loving wife. They knew Robin, too, and they believed she would strengthen me for the ministry, not only because of her similar loss, but also because of her strong and wholesome personality. She was remarkably equipped to meet my deep emotional needs. We certainly also considered Robin's needs. With all my heart I wanted to love and care for Robin. I wanted to be all that she needed. Dr. Smith counseled with her and was impressed with her maturity and her capacity to bring strong and wholesome qualities to the marriage. He felt that we would be good for each other.

I sought the advice of a number of other godly people whose wise counsel had been of infinite value to me on many occasions. A host of friends and associates affirmed me and encouraged me to marry Robin if I felt that God had brought us together.

Then I went to Cindy's family and told them about Robin. They will never know how much it meant to me when they gave, not just their approval, but their warmest wishes. . . their blessing. Those dear people knew I had loved Cindy with every fiber of my being during the years we'd been together and that I had given her everything I possibly could. They didn't feel it would be disrespectful or disparaging if I married again even though Cindy had been dead only seven months. They saw nothing to be gained by my languishing in the lap of depression and pity. They also understood my deep need for one woman to have and to hold.

It was time to tell my congregation about my plans with Robin. At that time I was preaching a series on the life of David, and the Sunday I planned to make my announcement my text was 1 Samuel 15. I presented the story of King David and Abigail. An angry David set out to avenge himself for Nabal's unkindness to him and his men. He vowed to kill every male in Nabal's family. Nabal's wife, Abigail, went out to meet David to plead for the innocent males, and also to exhort David, as God's man, to turn from vengeful bloodshed. David praised God for Abigail and accepted her good judgment. Later when Nabal died, David sent for beautiful, intelligent Abigail and asked her to become his wife.

"God has sent my Abigail," I told my church family following my message, "in the person of Robin Covington. As surely as God sent Abigail out to meet David, He has sent Robin to meet me in my time of need. Robin lost her fiance' about a year and three months ago. And she has, in the knowledge of like pain, reached out to lift me up.

"You are my family and I always told you I'd be up front with you. You know that Cindy and I were married for nearly twelve years, and we dated a long time before that. She was my best friend, and I loved being married to her. I never wanted to be single. And for most of these months since she's been gone, I would have called her back if there had been any way I could. But not now. God has given me the grace to leave her with Him and move on to another era in my life. Robin and I plan to be married within the next few months. Keith Moore summed it up as well as anybody could when he said, 'You compliment Cindy in wanting to repeat the happy life you had with her.'"

Robin and I never intended to marry as soon as we did. But it finally came down to the question: why not? All of the questions were answered. Honestly, before God we felt it was the right thing to do.

Our wedding was the same as anybody else's with the pressures of trying to please a lot of people. We wanted it to be beautiful and meaningful. I wanted it to be all that Robin had dreamed of because she had not been married before. Flanked by my fellow ministers and with Harry Smith performing the ceremony, Robin and I were married at New Hope Baptist Church on October 1, 1983. Hundreds of people came to be with us, including—God bless them—Cindy's mother, father, and sister.

The only hitch in the ceremony came when Robin, intending to promise me her best affections, misspoke herself and said, "I. . . give you all my best infections."

Dear God, what has she got that she didn't tell me about? I thought I checked everything!

Even though we were young, Robin and I had both weathered some heavy storms. As I took her hand on our wedding day, I knew other storms awaited us because life is like that. But I knew a greater thing: we both had discovered God's "treasures of darkness." We had seen His "riches in secret places." As we lit the unity candle, making two candles glow as one, heart spoke to heart against the backdrop of the soloist's words, "We will live out each day and turn our face toward a new tomorrow." Dr. Smith made the traditional presentation, "I present to you Dr. and Mrs. Dwight Reighard." Then he added, "Or to us, just Ike and Robin."

The congregation broke into spontaneous, affirming applause. Once again I knew that God was with me, and things were exactly as they should be. God sent Robin to be my wife.

Oh, God, You've given me so much. I only ask You for one more thing: a heart that is as grateful as it ought to be.

Chapter 14
Robin Speaks

The only way the miracle of my life can be understood is in understanding what God did in Robin's life as well. Because of this, I've asked her to tell her own story in her own words in this chapter.

There was no way I could have known that one day I would become Ike Reighard's wife, but even in the early days following Cindy's death, I felt strongly impressed to try to help him. I didn't understand my strong reaction to Ike's sorrow, but I kept seeing him as a part of my own healing.

I barely knew Ike and Cindy at the time of her death. I didn't even attend the funeral. Still, I hurt for Ike and prayed for him all that day. I knew what he was feeling because only months earlier, I'd been through the valley of the shadow myself.

I saw Phil for the first time when I was fourteen years old. We fell in love immediately. We dated for six happy years, and from day one of that span, we planned to get married.

Phil grew to be a great-looking, two-hundred-forty-five pound, six-foot-five young man. . . a real piece of work. He was a man's man and every inch a Christian gentleman. Phil and I did a lot of our growing up together. He a was nature-lover, fishing and hunting every chance he got. I followed him to the lakes and to the fields. I'd go anywhere just to be with him.

Sometimes we chopped wood to earn money for our dates. We went to dollar movies and "all-you-can-eat" smorgasbord meals. We spent time at his house and mine, because we loved each other's family. We were happy just sharing the simple things.

As the years passed, our love grew and we became emotionally dependent on our relationship. There was, however, one major difference between us. Phil was a Christian and I was not. I'd been bitter and hardhearted toward God since the death of my grandfather. I had loved and admired my grandfather. And I didn't want any part of a God who let good people die. I attended church with Phil sometimes, but since I was always struggling with why God permitted death, I never heard anything in the sermons except that we ought to get ready to die. The church represented death to me. And I cared about life!

Sometimes Phil annoyed me with his faith—it was so important to him. I tried to get him to do all kinds of compromising things. But he wouldn't. That boy even read his Bible on our dates! "Phil, put that thing up," I nagged to get his full attention. Then I'd call him "Lily White" to tease him about his good behavior and his faithfulness to God. A guileless guy—what a switch!

"Robin, won't you open your heart to God's love?" Phil often pleaded God's case. I knew my rebellion frustrated him. I didn't understand why he continued to pray for me. And though I didn't know what his prayers would do for me, I knew he would go on praying.

In August of 1978, Phil entered the University of Georgia on a football scholarship. We were separated for the first time. Faced with our separation, harder studies, unfamiliar people, and serving as a human punching bag on the football field, Phil found university life quite a challenge. I had a hard time with the separation too. I felt a tremendous loss when Phil was in Athens. I even tried dating a new guy once, but that only confirmed my love for Phil.

The summer before his sophomore year, Phil injured his knee while we were waterskiing. When fall practice

started, he tried his best to play on his bad knee. He
didn't want to give up. . . didn't want to fail those who
were counting on him. He endured braces, surgery, and
ongoing pain. But after the second hard blow to an
already ailing knee and more surgery, he had to relin-
quish all the dreams he'd built on playing football. With
a childlike quality, his faith held tough. True to form, my
protests were long and loud. "Good grief, Phil, how can
you still love God when He let you get hurt like that?
Your whole future's ruined."

"Well, I guess God has something in mind for me
besides playing football," he gave me a typical response.
He trusted God completely for whatever that something
else was.

Phil made a great Georgia Bulldog. Before graduat-
ing from Georgia, he captured the hearts of classmates,
teammates, and folks all over Athens. They called that
big moose "Mama" because he took care of everybody. He
made straight A's and signed a contract to be the student
assistant line coach for Georgia after he graduated.
Maybe, just maybe, his God was looking out for him
after all.

Plans for our future were coming together. We set
the date for our wedding. I bought my dress and chose
the bridesmaids' dresses. We planned the flowers and
the reception. After six years, my dream was finally
coming true. Phil and I were getting married!

As Phil's final year at Georgia closed, Coach Vince
Dooley invited the senior players and their wives or girl
friends to his home for his traditional end-of-the-year
party. It was one of the highlights of Phil's college days—
a casual steak supper in the coach's back yard. Graciously, Coach Dooley thanked the guys for what they'd
meant to the team and to the University of Georgia. He
encouraged them and pledged his interest and support
for their future endeavors. It was a sad time in a way
because the fellows had been through a lot in their four
years together. They'd shared the days of Herschel
Walker and a championship team. Justly proud of what
they'd accomplished, now each would go his own way.

Following the dinner, I spent the night with friends

in Athens. I awoke the next morning in my usual happy frame of mind. When I met Phil for breakfast, however, his mood was very different from mine. He was tense and pensive. Several times during the morning he hugged me and reminded me of something that was urgent to him. "Robin, I'm praying for us. And I'm praying that the wall around you will crumble and you will let God into your heart." Two or three times he spoke to me with a kind of finality. "I love you so much, Robin. I want you to remember, no matter what happens, I'll always be with you because you'll have me in your heart."

Why is he talking like this? I wondered, thinking he must still be feeling a touch of nostalgia from the night before.

When it came time for me to go, Phil walked me to the car. He kissed me and said goodbye more reluctantly than usual. When I got into the car, he made sure I fastened my seatbelt. Driving away, I looked back at and waved. I'd already started to miss him.

Saturday, June 5, dawned at Lake Lanier without a cloud in the sky. I had driven there to spend the weekend with my family. Phil was to join us later. It was good to be at the lake with my parents. I told them how much I loved and appreciated them, and I embraced their love for me. I put on my bathing suit and went out into the fresh air. The sun felt close and warm as it fell on my face. I wanted to celebrate the beauty of the morning, but the wariness in Phil's mood the day before had been contagious, and it disturbed my own contentment.

Mom, Dad, my sister Susan, and I took the boat out. After riding for a while, we stopped the motor and went over the side for a swim. All the time I thought about Phil and tried to wish away the hours until time for him to arrive. I wanted to see him and be sure everything was all right. Eventually we cranked up the boat and started back to the camp.

"I wonder what that's all about?" Daddy asked as he spotted some friends parked at our campsite. The shadow inside me darkened as I caught sight of them too.

We pulled the boat to shore and tied up. While I sat

frozen in the boat, the others got out to see what was going on.

Mother learned that someone was trying to get a message to us. She had a strong feeling that it was bad news, so she went immediately to the main gate to check it out.

I looked up in time to see her walking back toward me. Daddy and Susan stayed at the campsite. I climbed out of the boat calling out, "What's wrong? What's wrong?"

Suddenly, I knew why the apprehension had tugged at me ever since I'd left Phil. For the first time in my life, I cried out to God. "Lord Jesus, you've taken Phil away from me!" The look on my mother's face confirmed my fears.

Then I heard her voice. "Robin, Phil's had an accident." Reluctant, but determined to say it because it had to be said, she added, "Honey, he's dead."

Something crashed violently inside of me. My screams torc the summer air as I exploded out of control. "Phil! Phil! Phil!" Instinctively I started running. *Run! Run forever. . . run to where Phil is!* My intention was to run right over the rim of reality. But I didn't know how. Phil was dead, and I had to face it. That God has done it to me again!

Going to see Phil's family that night was the hardest thing I ever did. His mom, dad, sister Margaret, and brothers Warren and John were family to me. I thought my heart would break when I saw them. In love, clinging to each other, we shared the deepest kind of pain. We wept long and hard together. "I tried to save him, Robin. I did everything I could." A brokenhearted Warren struggled to assure me.

Warren had been working with Phil at the time of the accident, and he told me all that was known about what happened. They were baling hay. Phil was running the tractor and Warren was driving the truck. About lunchtime Warren took the truck in and waited for Phil to join him. When he didn't come, Warren went back to check on him. He found the tractor lying on its side with the motor still running. Phil lay unconscious on the ground nearby. He had been standing on the tractor watching it move along the ditch line. Somehow the tractor had kicked over. Phil fell off and the tractor rolled over him, crushing his ribs and breaking his neck. Warren frantically tried to revive him, but it was too late.

Dismal hours in the funeral home crept by. How impossible that Phil was lying motionless in a grey, satin-lined casket! I pinned a little pink rose on the lapel of his blue-grey jacket. In his pocket I tucked a bulldog figurine I had bought and forgotten to give him.

People came from everywhere to offer sympathy. I stayed by Phil and held his hand during the entire visitation. My heart and spirit spewed a morbid bitterness. *I wish they wouldn't stare at Phil like this. I wish they wouldn't even come by and look at him.*

I hated the sickening smell of the flowers. And I resented every attempt at consolation, especially the comments that made reference to God. I wanted to scream out my resentment: "Get out of my face! The God you're ramming down my throat took the most important thing in my life! And quit telling me how good Phil looks. He's cold as a fish and as hard as a rock. He's dead and he's never coming back!"

Phil's beloved grandfather brought the funeral message at the First Methodist Church in Fayetteville, Georgia—the church where we would have been married. If I had known how to look for it, I would have seen God's strength in Pepa Gray that day because he did a beautiful job. And though Phil was his fair-haired boy, the joy of his life, Pepa proclaimed with tearless voice the value of a Christian young man and the love of a God who saved him.

Following the service, hundreds of people joined us in the hour-long drive to Long Oak Cemetery. Just before we entered Long Oak, the entire procession was forced to stop and watch a phenomenal occurrence. Right in front of the procession, a beautiful white-tailed deer sauntered onto the road. He posed with lifted nose for several minutes, then gracefully walked away. It was an appropriate benediction for a young man who delighted in all of nature and its Maker, a man who "loved all of God's creatures, both great and small."

Susan, the only Christian in our family then, kept us afloat in the sea of darkness that followed Phil's death. Susan is a small girl in stature, but her devoted heart bore the weight of our grief as she continued to pray and trust God to see us through. She encouraged me to pray too, but I was insistent in my arrogance and rebellion. "Pray? You're crazy! I'm not praying to anything. God expects me to become a Christian through Phil's death? You've gotta be kidding!"

As time passed, my bitterness and grief deepened. My dread of everyday life overcame all reason. The dreary nights oppressed me so I couldn't sleep alone. My body would tremble all over, and I couldn't keep from crying aloud. I would get in bed with my parents in an effort to feel some security. I began to have a deep desire to take my own life and even tried to plan the best way to do it. With wicked boldness I shoved my face in God's face and taunted, "If You're so good, You'll strike me dead 'cause I don't want to live without Phil!"

Even though I tenaciously held to my angry grief, my parents were as patient and understanding as they knew how to be. They stood by me and did everything they could to help me adjust. I had wanted a bulldog to keep me company. Of course, bulldogs reminded me of Phil and University of Georgia days. My parents got me a precious little bulldog named Poopsie. Then they let me choose the family's summer vacation spot. After careful thought, I chose Arizona. I figured Arizona in mid-July would be pretty hot and miserable, and about the only thing that pleased me was seeing others suffer too.

One day when I was particularly unreasonable, I quarreled hysterically with my emotionally depleted mother. In what she felt was a last chance to save me, she slapped me across the face. The lick jolted me into a moment of reality. It was the first time in weeks I had really looked at my mother's face, and when I did, I saw there a grief and anguish that matched my own. *What is she going through?* I asked myself.

For the first time since Phil's death I came out of myself and considered my parents. They had suffered a great loss too. They loved Phil like a son. Now they felt that they were losing me. If I took my life, it would be more than they could stand. I just couldn't hurt them like that.

I'd been so stubborn in not wanting to reach out for help. I was used to being strong and independent and I didn't think I needed anybody else—I'd always been a winner. But facing the truth, I knew I was losing this time, and bringing my parents down with me. Although I hated the thought, it was time to give over, time to give in.

I found myself in the office of John Jenkins at New Hope Baptist Church. New Hope was Susan's church and she was sure John could help me. I sat stiffened in a chair across from John's desk. He listened intently as I poured out my desolation. "You've got to do something for me. If somebody doesn't help me, I won't be here next week." Then, I divulged the deepest desire of my heart, "I want eternal life because I want to see Phil again."

With grave concern, John told me that eternal life comes only through Jesus Christ and the acceptance of Him as God's Son, our Savior. If I would see Phil, I must see Jesus first. John made it plain that the matter would be settled in my will. I opened my heart to all that I heard. As John explained Christ's role, and mine, in salvation, I struggled to respond. I was not deliberately resisting, but something kept pushing against me.

John led me in the sinner's prayer. As I prayed to receive Christ, I continued to feel the oppression. I felt dizzy and heavy, as if some unseen force held me to the chair. The room became uncomfortably warm. I looked up from the prayer to see how John was. Distress engraved his face. His forehead was wet with perspiration and his shirt was soaked. He looked up at me. "Robin, there's something strange going on here. We've got to pray again."

We got down on our knees. John prayed again, asking God to set me free from Satan's grasp, to protect me, and give me wisdom and strength to become His child. Battling against the power of the adversary with conviction and sincerity, I asked Jesus Christ to come into my heart. And He did.

I stood to my feet in a room which was cool again. I felt relieved and lighter than I had in a long time, for the preponderant burden of hostility and rebellion had melted away. Assured that I belonged to God, I knew I would be His forever. And I would see Phil again—that was God's bonus. How odd the equation: My grandfather's death had driven me from God; Phil's death had drawn me to God. Phil was with the Lord. His prayers for me had been answered. Death was robbed its victory, denied its fiery sting.

Although my sorrow and yearning for Phil didn't end, I had a new strength in Christ. Life without Phil was still difficult. It was hard for me to go to church, hard to sit in a pew and hear an optimist like Ike Reighard tell me how wonderful life is. *Man, you don't know anything! I thought. You haven't lost anybody. If you had, you wouldn't be up there dancing around with the jollies saying, "God can put it back together.*

I really doubted that God would put things back together for me. How could He without bringing Phil back? Yet I tried to trust Him to help me in some way. And I went about the business of living. The night I heard about Cindy's death, I went to my room, angry at God again. I blurted out the same questions that had kept me in bondage so long. "How can You let a good person die? How can You take away from a godly man the one he loves most?"

I shut my door, sat in the dark, and prayed. I cried tears of agony that I'd been able to restrain in recent days. Everything I'd been through with Phil rushed back to bombard me—the same hurt, the same fury. But I was a child of God this time. And He came to me. "Robin, you're saying to Me that you are a Christian. And I'm saying to you that you are a survivor, a winner, and you're going to win this battle with sorrow. But you must give up Phil now. You must give him up to Me. You cannot have him in your life on earth—he is with Me."

I started to put away Phil's photographs. My room

had become a memorial to Phil Gray. Many keepsakes had to be put away, but I got the job done at God's instruction and in His strength. If I were to have a future, I must put away the past. After clearing away the mementoes that night, I came out of my room a new person. . . a person ready for life.

In subsequent days, I remembered hearing that following my salvation experience, John Jenkins told Ike he'd never been locked in a battle with Satan the way he was when he witnessed to me. And he'd added prophetically, "God surely must have something special in mind for that young lady!"

I didn't know then that the special assignment was to become Ike's wife. I wanted to help Ike overcome his grief, but being his wife was more of a challenge than I'd bargained for. When Ike and I developed a close relationship, I hurried to tell the Lord what I thought: "A preacher's wife! What a terrible thing to be!" I had my own stereotyped idea of a preacher's wife, and it wasn't something I cared to be, but after Ike and I fell in love, and the talk of marriage started, I got scared. It was time to set things straight with God on that point. "Lord, I believe You've made a mistake here. I've helped this man out, and we're friends. We're good friends. We're best friends. . . . I'll even admit I love him! But I don't want to marry him because I don't want to be a preacher's wife! You can change this thing around just any day now and lead me in another direction. I'm not going to wear bouffant hairstyles, purple polyester pantsuits, and little black slippers, and smile constantly. You're not talking to Miss Lily White. I'm me, God, and I can't be anybody else.

"If You want this preacher married, that's fine. But You've called up the wrong number here. There are a lot of girls out there who'd love to be a preacher's wife and I know You can locate one for Ike without any trouble. But please, Lord, don't look at me!"

I put in a request for a job transfer to another state thinking maybe God wouldn't get me there. But I never made the move. All I could hear from heaven was, "Robin, I want you to marry this man." All I could hear from Ike was, "Robin, I love you." I couldn't continue to resist them both.

Chapter15

Her Father's Joy

People have asked me, "When did you stop grieving for Cindy and the baby?" My answer to that question is, "Never." Almost every day something reminds me of a woman who gave me fifteen years of her life. And though it may have appeared that I got over it too soon, the truth is that I will never get over it entirely. My life changed, but the past will always be a part of the present.

The beauty is that Robin understands the altered life because she also walked away from a newly made grave. She also has scars and wounds that freshen at the touch of reminiscence. Phil is still a part of her life just as Cindy is a part of mine.

Only God could have put us together so perfectly. Only a woman like Robin could understand the thrust of new pain I feel sometimes when I see a girl with red hair, linger to look at a child the age mine would have been, or hear some other whisper from the past. We both have sweet memories "pressed between the pages of our minds." Both of us know the nostalgia that rolls in when a favorite song is played, a favorite restaurant comes into view, or a special anniversary or birthday approaches. We can empathize, each with the other.

Robin not only understands my heart, but she encourages me to tell my story at every opportunity. She wants me to share hope with others who have lost loved ones by telling how God watched over me in my loss and loneliness. It is her joy, as well as mine, to proclaim His matchless grace in restoring me and blessing me a hundredfold.

Robin and I are often amused at the way we're tempted to deify Cindy and Phil. We sometimes refer to them as "Saint Cindy" and "Hero Phil" to remind ourselves that we tend to think of them the way we want to, and not the way they really were. It's a trick of human nature, when we lose a loved one, to remember only a composite that we create in our minds. But it isn't fair to Robin for me to think of Cindy as having been perfect in this world. I've learned to live in the present, look to the future, and cherish the past.

I told Robin early on that I would like for us to try to begin our family just as soon as we were married. I was already in my thirties, and I wanted to be able to walk across the field without a walker when my daughter became homecoming queen. "What makes you so sure you'll have a daughter?" Robin wanted to know. "And how do you know she'll be homecoming queen?"

Well, I didn't know how I knew I'd have a daughter. I just knew. But the homecoming queen part was easy. If I had to bribe somebody, I would do it. If I had to start my own school, I would do that. I figured no matter what it took, she would be homecoming queen.

Robin agreed that we should have a baby right away. And one month following our wedding, she became pregnant. Her pregnancy was difficult in the early stages. When Christmastime came, she was quite ill. In addition to the usual sickness of early pregnancy, she began running a fever and having pain in her back. While other family members opened Christmas presents and enjoyed a festive dinner, a sick and sagging Robin lay flat on the sofa.

I remember sitting on the floor close to her. I held her hand, stroked her hair, and attempted to encourage her. "Next Christmas is going to be different. You'll see. I'll make it the best Christmas you ever had." I couldn't help but cry, as I prayed, "Oh, God, why can't it ever be easy?"

Her obstetrician advised us to consult her family physician. At this point we decided to get in touch with a team of doctors from our church, Pat and Rebecca Anders. Both the doctors Anders are OB/GYN specialists and fine Christian doctors. Dr. Pat graciously consented to see Robin. Immediately he diagnosed a kidney infection and prescribed treatment. Soon Robin was okay. We believe his timely detection probably saved the pregnancy.

The Anders were so kind and thoughtful, we decided to keep Robin under their care. And that arrangement was made to order! It was sort of like an OB tag team— a doctor for Robin and one for me. She got her blood pressure taken; I got my blood pressure taken. She got weighed; I got weighed. As Dr. Rebecca looked after me, I became the only daddy in baby-having-history with his own obstetrician.

Except for that kidney infection, Robin did fine with her pregnancy. I was a little more trouble. But the Anders kept me assured that everything was going to be all right. I never quit thanking God for those precious friends.

Throughout our days of waiting, Robin continued to accompany me on my speaking engagements. She glowed with the natural radiance of a mother-to-be, and I was proud of her. The only negative thing I can remember was her nonnegotiable craving for egg foo yong. She wanted that stuff night and day, but egg foo yong three times a day began to get old to me!

Our big night finally arrived. I came home from performing a wedding on a Saturday evening. As I entered the house, Robin's mom greeted me with the announcement, "Robin's water broke." Instant panic!

Impulsively I jumped into cleaning the house. Housework is not my usual thing, and the house wasn't even dirty. But that didn't matter; it was something to do and I moved into fast action. I hurled dishes into the dishwasher, then attacked the fridge tossing out dozens of Chinese take-out cartons. I pitched pillows, jerked bed sheets, crammed clothes in the washing machine, and started on the bathrooms. I dove into bathtubs with Comet Cleanser, scrubbed sinks, scoured toilets, and mopped floors. I did anything I could to stay busy. I knew if I didn't, I'd have to think about how scared I was.

Out of fear and concern for Robin's pain, I cried all the way to South Fulton Hospital. It was about 12:30 A.M. when we checked in, and she was ushered into the labor room. We hadn't planned for me to be with her for the delivery. Robin felt that having a baby and taking care of me at the same time would be a little too much. She decided in favor of the baby.

After she was prepped, the nurses let me go back to see her. Just as I walked through the door, I was greeted by one of them. "You're Ike Reighard, aren't you?" I told her that I was, and thanked God for a friendly face.

She explained that she'd attended New Hope Baptist Church many times, and she knew the tragedy I'd experienced with Cindy. "There's another nurse here who knows you too," she said. Those two nurses kept me encouraged during the entire waiting time.

In addition to having two nurses who knew me and what I'd gone through before, we had the phenomenal privilege of being the only couple in South Fulton Hospital for delivery that night. We got total attention. God was looking after the smallest detail.

I predicted that the baby would be born at 3:30 A.M. because we both woke up every morning of her pregnancy at that time. At 3:45 Dr. Rebecca came out and congratulated me. The baby had been born at 3:36.

She gave me the happy news that everything had gone well—Robin and the baby were fine. She told me I could go back and see them, but before she got the words out of her mouth, I was halfway down the hall. Just as I reached Robin's room, I saw her and the baby on the gurney being pushed toward me. I hurried to see for myself that they were okay. I checked Robin first. And the baby, all red and newborn, lay on her stomach. Both of them were all right! It was over and they were okay! Overwhelmed with relief and gratitude, I dropped to my knees. "Thank You, Lord. Thank You. Thank You, Lord." I could hardly believe it was true.

The nurse held up the baby for me to see. Still on my knees, and trying to see through my tears, I asked, "What is it?" The only thing the infant was wearing was a little stocking cap. I could have sworn I would know a little girl when I saw one, but for some reason I kept repeating, "What is it? What is it?" And the nurses kept insisting, "It's a girl. It's a girl." But how could I have immediately taken in the miraculous answer to my deepest dreams?

First, I noticed that, tiny and wrinkled, she bore an unusual resemblance to E.T. At the same time, she was the most beautiful thing I'd ever seen. She was so alert and bright-eyed—a ten on the Apgar Scale! Even at birth it was as if she could look right into my heart and know that I was her father. We hit it off from the start, and the first time I held her I experienced some extravagant new emotions, great surges of protection. . . love. . . adoration . . . pride. This was my daughter!

Robin and I named our little girl Abigail, a name that was already precious to me. We chose it for its beauty and for its perfect meaning—her father's joy!

After I knew for certain that everything was all right and Robin was resting, I went out to get some breakfast. My parents, Robin's parents, and some friends went with me. Stepping outside in the rosy-hued dawn, I thought: "Now this is going to be the most beautiful day that has ever been, July 29, 1984." Yet I couldn't help thinking about that evening a lifetime ago when I'd walked away from another hospital. In the same sky, I had seen the sun set on my dream, and my life lay in pieces all around me.

But today was a new day. The sun was rising on a bright, new dream. Once again I was full of hope. With His fatherly regard, God had restored my life and fulfilled my hope. He had proven His Word. "Delight yourself in the LORD; And He will give you the desires of your heart" (Psalm 37:4 NASB). I praised Him and agreed with the psalmist, "Weeping may endure for a night, but joy comes in the morning" (Psalm 30:5b).

On Monday I warned Robin, "I'm not going to be here early tomorrow. But I'll be along after I've done some errands."

The next morning I went shopping. I found a wonderful shop at Lenox Square that was having a sale. I bought clothes for the baby in several sizes because it was the only way I could buy as many as I wanted to. There were dresses for Abigail and dresses for Robin. I'd been afraid to count too much on a flawless delivery, but now it was real and I could celebrate. My joy and gratitude were so boundless that they overrode my economic restraint.

When I showed up at the hospital, I had to have help carrying in all the stuff I'd bought. In Robin's room we had festivities the likes of which that hospital had never seen before. Many of the hospital personnel crowded in to see the baby's fashion show. A new era of life was beginning for me. I was Abigail's father!

With the words of Habakkuk I praised the God of my strength. He had given me "hind's feet on high places," and He had brought me over the mountain. (See Hab. 3:18-19.)

Chapter 16

"He Giveth Again"

God so completely reconstructed my life, it would seem nothing else could add to my restoration. Yet the God of surprises had another gift for Robin, Abigail, and me—the sensational gift of Danielle.

The entrance of Danielle into Reighard family history began on a very routine day. In the spring of 1988, I received a telephone call from Stan Hill, pastor of the Covenant Baptist Church in Bristol, Tennessce. Stan was calling to invite me to help with an evangelistic conference his church had planned for the following September. The weekend he had in mind was the last open weekend on my calendar. I didn't know Stan, but he sounded so enthusiastic and excited about what was going on in his church, I hated to turn down his invitation. "I'd really like to come," I told him, "but to tell you the truth, my schedule requires that I be away from my wife so much this year. I just don't feel I should add anything that would take me out of town." When Stan realized that separation from Robin was the main difficulty, he asked if she also took speaking engagements. When he learned she did, he included her in the invitation. It was a good arrangement, and we accepted with gratitude.

The September dates came in a hurry. Robin and I boarded a commuter plane and flew into the Johnson City airport right on schedule. When we got to the baggage claim, we found that some of our luggage was missing, so I went to check on it while Robin sat down on a suitcase that had arrived okay and continued to read her *Glamour* magazine. (Robin has these unusual daily quiet times she spends with *Glamour* magazine or the *Speigel Catalog*.) Just as I returned to her, I looked up and saw a man and woman and three girls coming our way. I knew immediately the man was Stan Hill—when you've been in the ministry as long as I have, you can spot a preacher a mile away. As we introduced ourselves, Robin and I noticed that Stan, his wife, Pam, and two of the girls bore a decided family resemblance to each other. They all had sandy hair and blue eyes. However, the other child, six-year-old Danielle, had dark hair and skin, and eyes that looked like two Milk Duds. After looking at her for a moment, I thought, *This child doesn't look like the rest of the family. In fact, she looks just like Robin!*

In the course of the next two days, we came to love the Hills. Stan and Pam both had a genuine concern for people, and it was reflected in their happy children. They had five children—four of their own plus Danielle, and we had a great time with all of them. In our limited leisure time, we all climbed into their van and took off together to see the area. I rode in the back with the kids so I could sing and play with them. If I'm with a group of four or more kids, I can usually create a riot within fifteen minutes and that is just what I did with the Hill children. All of them responded to me except Emily, the baby, who couldn't quite make up her mind. Danielle zipped under my arm right away and stuck there like a piece of velcro. To my chagrin, she told me I reminded her of her grandfather. (That was the only thing I didn't like about the kid!) Seriously, though, Robin, Danielle, and I got to be good buddies in the short time we had together.

In the services at Covenant Baptist Church I endeavored, as I always do, to preach in a way that is understandable to children. If children don't understand what I'm saying, adults probably won't either. After fifteen years of preaching, I still find the greatest gratification when a child hears, understands, and accepts Christ. At the close of the second service, I went out into the vestibule to visit with the folks as they were leaving. While I was there, a woman came up and asked, "Did you know Danielle was saved tonight?" I hadn't seen her come forward and didn't know, but when I heard about it, I went back inside to look for her. I located Danielle in the counseling area. She looked up at me with her extraordinary brown eyes, and I saw round, fat tears glide slowly down her cheeks. They were tears of her joy in the sweetness of finding the Savior of her soul. I picked her up, hugged her, and told her how proud I was of her and how excited I was that she was going to be living her life for Jesus. She was so special to me. I was not present for the physical birth of Danielle, but I was there for her spiritual birth and that will always hold significant meaning for me.

As Robin and I developed a closer relationship with the Hills, they told us Danielle's story. Her mother, Stan's cousin, had been struggling to bring up six children in a single-parent home. When Danielle was four years old, her mom had an automobile accident that left her in a coma from which she had not recovered. Richard Hill, Danielle's grandfather, became the legal guardian of the children and thus responsible for the future of all the children. Mr. Hill cares for his wife who is confined to a wheelchair, so it was not possible for this couple to undertake the rearing of six children. As hard as it was for him, he had to decide to separate the children in order to find homes for them. Stan and Pam lovingly took Danielle, and she had been with them for two years. As Robin and I learned what Danielle had been through, we felt an emotional bond with her. She was only six years old and already she knew the heavy weight of grief.

When the conference was over and we were ready to leave, we told Stan and Pam that if Mr. Hill ever decided permanent adoption was the best alternative for Danielle and if he and Pam felt that it was God's will for her, we would like them to consider us as possible parents. They thanked us and that was about all that was said. We left Bristol with an unexpected, subtle anticipation because we felt that somehow Danielle's destiny might be entwined with our own.

In the months that followed our introduction to Danielle, Robin and I prayed that God would guide all of us as we considered her future. We were keenly aware that we were dealing with the life of a child and that the most important thing at stake was God's will for Danielle. As we went through the Christmas holidays, we kept thinking about her, wondering what her Christmas was like, wanting to send her a gift but deciding against it. We put her picture out and continued to think about what it would be like if she were living in our home. As we thought of her and prayed for her, we began to feel in our hearts that one day God would give her to us. From time to time we were tempted to call Stan and ask if Mr. Hill had made any decision with regard to adoption. Then we'd say, "No, if God wants to open that door, He'll open it. We don't want to push on it."

We tried to be sensitive to the way the Hills felt. They were deeply committed to the Lord, and I felt that if this were honestly God's will, He would confirm it first to them. They had been excellent parents to Danielle and had brought her through a difficult transition period. They'd taught her well, spiritually and psychologically. They adored her and she loved them too, so any thought of losing her from their own home and family was painful for them. We knew they would do exactly what God wanted them to do, and they would do it in His timing. Our job was to wait and pray. After all, we could have other children, adoption was not a last resort for us, but I had always wanted to adopt a little girl—not an infant, but an older child—and I believed Danielle just might be the one.

A couple of weeks after we left Bristol, Stan wrote me a letter asking me to come back and help with some additional evangelistic meetings the following spring or summer. For some reason the letter was mislaid in my office and didn't get answered. This is unusual because I make a point of always answering my mail. One day, approximately four months later, I was going through some things on my desk, and Stan's letter surfaced.

Totally puzzled, I asked Sandy, my secretary, if she knew how the letter could have suddenly showed up after so long a time. Neither of us could account for where it had been, but I answered it immediately, making apologies to Stan for such a tardy response. In the letter I asked if he would say hello to our little girl, Danielle.

About four days later, Stan called and said, "Ike, you may think what I'm going to tell you is strange, but Pam and I had started praying that if God wanted Danielle to come live with you, you would contact us. On the third day of that specific prayer, I received your letter. We believe it was God's way of telling us to talk with you further about her."

He went on to tell me that Danielle's mother's condition had worsened, and her coma had been pronounced irreversible. Any hope of putting the family back together was lost, and one of the children had already been adopted. Stan and Pam felt the time had come when careful thought needed to be given to making permanent arrangements for Danielle too. They wanted so much to keep her with them, but God had given them four children of their own, and they were not sure He intended for them to have Danielle permanently. Stan was calling to see what we were feeling and thinking, and he offered to let her come and visit us for a couple of weeks.

Crying with joy and anticipation, I hung up, called Robin and told her what Stan had said. All I could hear through the receiver was Robin sobbing out the words, "I just know she's supposed to come and live with us! I just know she's supposed to come and live with us!"

Danielle's visit would give us all a chance to test the waters. The Hills were concerned about us as well as Danielle. They knew that bringing another person into a family creates a lot of new responsibility. When we accept that person, we accept whatever baggage they bring—and I'm not talking about suitcases. Even with a child, there can be a lot of baggage, and Danielle had not had an easy time. We all agreed that after a brief visit, she would be going back to Bristol. Although Danielle did not know everything that had been discussed, she knew that consideration was being given to her coming to live with us. She was assured that nothing would be decided against her will.

Abigail, four years-old by this time, was also a vital part of the decision. We promised her that if she were not happy with the prospect, we would not proceed. She prayed with us as we tried to remain sensitive to the way God would lead our family. Abby had a rather precocious sensitivity for people in need because, in addition to her exposure to my ministry, she had seen the ministry Robin had with deprived families. Even at her young age, she knew that people sometimes struggle with pain and problems. She was also keenly aware that our family was blessed, and she understood our concept of burden-sharing.

Our household was filled with excitement as Danielle came to visit. I was impressed with Robin's prayers as they centered around her possible role as Danielle's mother. "God, if she's meant to be mine, let me love her in the same way I love Abigail." Robin wanted to help Danielle with her bath, her hair. . . her personal care in the way a loving mother does. After all, Danielle was a six-year-old stranger, not a child born to her, and Robin wanted to be sure she could embrace the servanthood of mothering Danielle, and not feel it strange or unusual. That seemed to be her test for determining whether or not she was right for Danielle. "God answered my prayer completely," Robin said later. "It was as if she had always been mine. And my heart skipped at least four beats the first time I heard her call me 'Mama.'" Robin and I both found parenting Danielle as natural as parenting Abigail.

We were tempted to pour out our love by showering Danielle with presents while she was with us, but we didn't want to influence her feelings or attempt to buy her love. Although she is not a materialistic child, we knew if we weren't careful, we could dazzle her with material things. Our family had never been happier than during those two weeks Danielle was with us. We played together and worshipped together as the time flew by. We need never have had any concern about the two girls bonding. They were sisters from the start. Danielle's sweet, kind spirit and Abby's healthy, happy disposition made for an easy blend. They loved each other with no threat of jealousy between them—we knew that had to be from the Lord!

When the visit came to its inevitable end, we had to return Danielle to the Hills. They were coming to Marietta for a conference and the plan was for us to meet them there. Robin and I woke up the morning of the return with a silent dread dogging our spirits. We managed to hold together on the way and through the meeting, but we cried all the way home. We vowed that we would never put ourselves through another experience of togetherness, then separation. I kept trying to word a prayer, "God, what if we don't get her, when I am so sure. . . ." And then, I would start again, "God, if this can be in Your will. . . ." Finally I faced it: if it was in His will, I didn't need to help. I clung to that confidence.

A few long weeks later, the Hills told us they had talked with Danielle and she felt that our home would be home for her. Her grandfather, who had really left it up to Stan, was pleased that she would be in a Christian home. It seemed that letting us adopt her was the right thing to do. I hurt for Stan and Pam. The only way they could give her up was in their consecration to God and their total commitment to His will for themselves and for Danielle. It was one of the hardest decisions of their life, and it bore out the age-old truth that sometimes the right thing to do is the hardest thing to do. Stan and Pam gave up Danielle because, before God, they felt it was right.

Robin and I saw so much in Danielle, and we wanted to be her doorway from the rain. We had lost a lot, we had struggled, but we had come out as winners. We wanted to help Danielle win too. We wanted to give back to life because life had joyfully given us each other, Abigail, and so much more. We felt that in Danielle we could make a contribution to what is good and kind in this world. She was yearning for a permanent home and family, and we provided that, but we don't feel we've done her a favor. In fact, the opposite is true. We are the ones who were favored—we needed her. We almost felt selfish when she came because we wanted her so desperately. Danielle is a sensitive child who loves extravagantly, just as we do, so her only hesitation in coming to us was her concern that the Hills would think she didn't love them. She knew that she was going to miss them, especially at first. I believe that adoption, in the hands of God, is every bit as miraculous as giving birth to a child. In one sense, it is even more wondrous. God's wisdom in choosing and putting together people whose paths have never crossed is remarkable. And, I remind myself, if it were not for God's adoption plan, none of us would be His children.

The day we went to bring Danielle home, I was filled with a whole mush of emotions—excitement, gratitude, happiness, some apprehension. But a sense of completion dominated everything else I felt. We pick up Danielle on March 4, 1989, six years and one day following the burial of my first child. Six years and one day. . . and that's seven. There's always been something significant and holy about the number seven.

We loaded Danielle and her belongings in the car and headed for Lenoir City, Tennessee, and a family gathering with lots of Robin's folks. It seemed right that Robin's family be on hand to help us welcome Danielle because all her relatives had been great to us. And Robin's parents, "Granny" and "Grumps," are such wonderful grandparents. I've come to love and appreciate them in a great way in the last six years. After that party, we traveled happily down highway 175 to show off the new granddaughter to Ernest and Ruthie Reighard in Dallas, Georgia. Oh yes, Danielle had herself quite a family!

When we left Dallas, we headed toward Fayetteville, Georgia. Danielle, as excited as we were, couldn't sit still. In her heart of hearts she too felt completed. She knew that, at long last, God had turned her footsteps home. She jumped up and down, beating her hand on the dashboard saying over and over again, "I'm home. I'm home. I'm finally home!"

I buried Cindy and the baby on March 3, 1983. We

left to pick up Danielle to come live with us on March 3, 1989. Later the lawyer gave us a copy of the Petition for Adoption, and as we were driving back from his office, Robin was reading it. Suddenly, she said, "Ike, you're not going to believe this: Danielle's mother had her accident on March 3, 1987." No wonder I feel that she is a piece of the puzzle of my life.

In recent months we've made adjustments of different kinds, and we've experienced the stresses that go with normal family life. But there's an awful lot of love in the Reighard home. There's manifold appreciation for the family bond and for the goodness of a God named Father who never quits giving. In a song called "He Giveth More Grace," Annie Johnson Flint talks about the abundance of grace God gives for the times of affliction. She talks about the strength He gives in the hard places; and how, when we reach the end of our hoarded resources, the Father's giving has only begun. The song closes with words that describe the generous God of my life's journey.

> His love has no limit,
> His grace has no measure,
> His power has no boundary known to men;
> For out of His infinite riches in Jesus,
> He giveth, and giveth, and giveth again![1]

Chapter 17

Memory, The Scribe of the Soul

God taught me things in my experience of loss and grief that I could never have learned any other way. He gave me an entirely different perspective on life, and He created in me a deep desire to share what I've learned with others who suffer in a similar way. As I continue this writing of my story, I wonder how many who read my words are going through a time of painful loss. If this is the case for you, I want you to know that my heart goes out to you. I will be praying for the readers of my work, so, dear friend, I will be praying for you. And part of my prayer will be that God will speak to you through the insights he gave to me.

It may sound elementary, but one concept that became mine in a very real way is that I must concentrate on *who God is* and not on *what He does*. When I hold the Lord Jesus Christ as the most important thing in my life, all other events—happy or sad—find their proper places. It is my prayer that as you struggle, you, too, will concentrate on who God is and find the same comfort. God is your loving Father, and He is in control of your life. He will never abandon you. As you bear your pain, give God a chance to work in your heart and mind, making alterations where they need to be made, and your outcome will be a positive one.

Your loss, no doubt, left you with a host of memories. Some are wonderful; some you wish you didn't have.

Learning to look at memories in a positive light was an exceptional help to my healing, and I believe it will help you too. One night in the early weeks after Cindy died, I was at home alone. I sat at my desk trying to prepare a sermon for Sunday morning. After finally starting to concentrate on the message, I was working away pretty good. I thought of a scripture I wanted to use but couldn't remember the reference. Cindy always had a commanding knowledge of the Scriptures, so out of habit, I spun around in my chair and called out, "Cindy, where do you find. . . ." My voice suddenly halted as the brutal truth struck me once again. Cindy will not answer me. Not tonight, not ever again.

A new surge of pain ricocheted through me. Fresh tears stung my eyes and ran down in profusion. I slumped over my desk, put my head on my arms, and let the tears pour. At times, when I was alone, I allowed myself to cry as long and hard as I needed to. The pain and weeping seemed to come from parts of my being that I didn't even know I had. These episodes of weeping invariably dredged up more memories.

The psalmist said, "I call to remembrance my song in the night; I meditate within my heart, And my spirit makes diligent search" (Ps. 77:6). That is exactly what we do. . . we remember and we search. We search for things that relieve our guilt, we search for things that assure us that the lost loved one was happy. . . we search for all kinds of hints that everything was okay. Part of God's "sufficient grace" is manifested in the strength that memory can bring to our souls, if we're careful to use memory in an advantageous way.

Rabindranath Tagore, an Indian poet, penned, "In the shady depth of life are the lonely nests of memories that shrink from words." Memories can be indescribably painful, but even in the hurting we may find that happy memories are a resting place from the heaviness of sorrow. Aristotle called memory "the scribe of the soul." It is the golden thread that links past thoughts and events to the present mind. To be sure, it saves both trash and treasure, but I believe we can choose to remember the best, then attempt to give the rest to God and let it go. A graceful spirit will make a good memory in the heart out of a bad memory in the head. God gives to you and me that needed grace as we open up to it, so don't be afraid to think and remember. To refuse to do so is to practice an unhealthy denial.

I'm not saying that all this rationale came to me when I was in deep sorrow. I can say it now, years later, and wish I had understood it more clearly then. Even as I share my experience in this writing, the events seem to have more purpose. They make more sense than they did at the time. Our memories can bring pleasure and comfort if we take a positive attitude. Conversely, if we dwell on the bad experiences, our memories can become like weird, black ghosts haunting us and making our hearts condemn us. I did not want that to happen to my memories of Cindy. She was too happy in life to be remembered morbidly. I remembered her wit and her zest for life. She could make me roll with laughter.

Once in Hawaii we went into a cookie shop. With her exaggerated southern drawl, Cindy gave her order, "I want some macadamia nut cookies, please." Each word she spoke came out with about five syllables. A curious man standing nearby looked up at her and said, "You must be from Texas." "Oh," came Cindy's innocent reply, "do people from Texas like macadamia nut cookies?"

I never let her forget that one! And I didn't forget it either. Filed in my memory bank, it has become a happy part of my past—a past that I now realize prepared me for what was to come. My memories have served me in a number of ways, and one of these is being able to see God piloting my journey all along the way as I recall specific incidents of my life.

Being transplanted as a small boy from the mountains to a big city taught me a good lesson: people aren't all alike. At that time, I was the one who was strangely different, and feeling different gave me a sensitivity that would carry over into adulthood.

Other events that helped develop my God-given gift for seeing life in wide-screen technicolor were also a part of the preparation for my future. As a child I found great pleasure in a myriad of things that represented excitement and adventure. The whole idea of flying fascinated me. I flew my kite as high as the wind would carry it and as long as daylight permitted. In my fantasies, I pointed my hands like Superman, left the earth and went wherever I pleased. Always a dreamer, I rode the clouds in the daytime and touched the stars at night.

I loved color and spent hours peering into my kaleidoscope, looking through pieces of colored glass or studying rainbows. At Christmastime, I found that if I crossed my eyes when I looked at the Christmas tree, I could double its shimmering lights. I learned that I could make life more fun by spraying it with some paint and tossing a little glitter on it. A supportive family who encouraged both my boyish love of life and my God-given polychromatic attitude contributed to an undefeatable inner confidence: I am of value. I was born to be happy. And somewhere there's a kingdom waiting for me.

This strong sense of personal value and destiny helped me through my time of grief. You may not possess such a specific sense of destiny, but you can be sure that God has put in you exactly what you need for the times of your life, including bereavement. You do have a future, and He will provide new life and good surprises as you continue your pilgrimage.

Hold your memories close, memories of your absent loved one and other memories as well. You will be able to see God's patterns and purpose—He has been working with you all the time. Some of the memories are painful, I know. Some are filled with resentment, others may be lined with disappointment or guilt. The bad times have probably become larger than life, but you might need to think about them too, being careful to keep in mind that all human relationships are shot through with misunderstanding, mistreatment, and mistakes.

In the *Complete Speaker's and Toastmaster's Library* compiled by Jacob M. Braude, I read these words: "Memory was given to mortals so that they might have roses in December."[1] I think that is a beautiful way to put it. My roses of remembrance never lose their fragrance. The inscription of Cindy's memory on my soul is for my good. To believe otherwise would mean that she did not make a positive contribution to my life. God and I both know better than that.

It's interesting to note how many times God asks us to employ our memories. He told us to remember Him, His commandments, His words, His great acts, His mercies, and His sabbath. And ultimately Jesus said, "Remember Me." A deliberate effort to remember Christ when the heart is broken strengthens the soul on which His love and comfort are forever scribed.

Chapter 18

The Heavenly Truth

The word bereave means to be deprived of something that is necessary or to have a valuable possession taken away, especially by force. Bereavement follows the loss of something precious. Bereavement, then, can be the result of a death, a divorce, or a relationship broken in some other way. It may also be brought about by experiences such as miscarriage, or loss of home, job, health, or youth. There is a kind of grief associated with rape, certain surgeries, moving from familiar places and people, and even less severe occurrences.

I realize that our Lord does not meet the needs of everybody's bereavement in the same way He met mine. He restored me in a unique way—He gave me another wife, other children. But God does not work the same in every case of loss. Many people who lose a spouse prefer not to remarry. Many lose a loved one whose role cannot be duplicated. And sometimes that which is lost or destroyed simply cannot be replaced. Our losses differ and our needs differ. Although God dries our tears in different ways, He has a restoration plan for everyone who grieves.

Victorious Christian living is, after all, believing that God will choose the best path for us, and daring never to choose our own. It is abandoning ourselves to Him in obedience and appropriating His promises, remembering that the Master has His own design for the

finished product that each of us can become.
Proverbs 3:5-6 bears out this concept:

> Trust in the LORD with all your heart,
>   And lean not on your own understanding;
> In all your ways acknowledge Him,
>   And He shall direct your path.

When we trust God, our paths are directed and our future is secured. When we abandon ourselves in this way, we get a bigger picture of who we are in the light of God's plan. Grief teaches us lessons that nothing else can teach us. It is true that grief must run its course, but we can adopt certain positive mindsets or attitudes that will help us do our "grief work" and also help us mature as children of God. The synopsis, however simple or complex it may appear, is that peace and better understanding come when we release ourselves to a God who is willing and able to take good care of us in all things.

As our grief gets us thinking about God's overall plan and how we fit into His universal will, we begin to have a new perspective. We give new thought to eternity and more consideration to what happens when this life is over, realizing that if we invest only in temporal things (and that is our tendency) eventually we will be bankrupt. As Christians we are comforted in the knowledge that heaven is our destination and we are merely travelers on our way. Paul says, "Reaching forward to those things which are ahead, I press toward the goal for the prize of the upward call of God in Christ Jesus" (Phil. 3:13-14). If we are bound to the earthly, we lose sight of "those things which are ahead. . . the prize." But grief causes us to focus on eternity, our reunion with loved ones, and the completion of our union with God. This perspective gives us ongoing hope when the path of our journey goes through trouble and sorrow. It was especially precious to me at the time of Cindy's death.

When my friend, Nelson Price, learned that Cindy had died, he called me on the telephone. "You know, Ike," he said in that beautiful, resonant voice of his. "Cindy is with the one Person who loved her more than you did."

His statement encouraged me because I had not thought of it quite that way.

I was glad Nelson did not quote Romans 8:28 to me just at that moment, although that verse meant much to me later on. When Cindy died, I was sure Romans 8:28 was a misprint or a bad translation. It didn't seem to me that God was working through all things for my good. That day I needed something simple to hold to, something new to think about. My love and care for Cindy was human. . . it was the best I could do. But she had moved on to enjoy perfect love and care, and Nelson's remark reminded me of that.

I was able to settle in my mind and heart that Cindy and the baby were with their loving and caring Lord. My life, and Cindy's too, was based on the truth of the death, burial, and resurrection of Jesus Christ and His promise of an eternal home for those who believed in Him. I was comforted by Jesus' own words, "In My Father's house are many mansions; if it were not so, I would have told you. I go to prepare a place for you. And if I go and prepare a place for you, I will come again and receive you to Myself; that where I am, there you may be also (John 14:2-3).

Cindy was in heaven because she believed and accepted God's loving invitation in John 3:16: "For God so loved the world that He gave His only begotten Son, that whoever believes in Him should not perish but have everlasting life."

The baby was with God because our heavenly Father loves and accepts innocent children. Of course I wondered what the baby looked like, what kind of personality he had. (I just felt in my heart the baby was a boy.) After all, the baby left a void, too, even though I never saw him. As I grieved over the loss of my child, I turned often to 2 Samuel 12 and read the story of David and his son. David mourned the illness of his son. And when the son died, David arose from his mourning, washed and anointed himself, changed his clothes, and went to the house of the Lord to worship. I received encouragement from his words, "I shall go to him but he shall not return to me" (2 Sam. 12:23).

I believe that my child will grow and flourish in a better world than this—a land of sunshine and beauty, a land without tears and sadness. He will know only perfection, with a loving Father in a pain-free world.

Thinking of my loved ones brought heaven so close to me. I thought more about life after death than I ever had before. With all my heart I believe Cindy and my baby were escorted immediately by angels right into the presence of the Lord Jesus Christ. I know you're expecting me to say how inexplicable her joy must have been when she saw Him. And I do believe that, but let me tell you something else—Jesus was glad to see Cindy too! He loves her so much He gave His life for her and He was glad to see her arrive home. Because of Cindy's trust in Christ, heaven was her real home for years before she was able to reach its gates and "be like Him," and "see Him as He is" (1 John 3:2).

I also believe when Jesus said to the thief on the cross, "Today you will be with Me in Paradise," He meant exactly that. And when Paul said, "to be absent from the body is to be present with the Lord" (2 Cor. 5:8), he was perpetuating that same truth. Because Jesus was resurrected from the dead, so was Cindy. I believe her resurrection was as rapid as the twinkling of an eye. If you will permit me a little imagination here, I want to tell you how I can picture Cindy's homegoing. I know what she thought. You see, every time Publishers Clearing House had a sweepstakes, Cindy entered. At that glorious moment when she opened her eyes in the middle of the most beautiful place she'd ever seen, she thought, *I won! I won! I won! I finally won the sweepstakes!* Among many other things, Cindy and I shared a sense of humor. I believe her next thought was, *Boy, wait till Ike sees this!*

The hope I have in Christ's promise of a happy eternity kept me sane in those grieving days. I kept reminding myself that we do not "sorrow as others who have no hope" (1 Thess. 4:13). We do have every hope in the resurrection of Jesus Christ and thus in our own resurrection. There was an odd excitement in realizing that Cindy already knew the full meaning of that. She was already discovering at least in part what Paul meant when he quoted to the Corinthians the verse from Isaiah 64:4: "Eye has not seen, nor ear heard, Nor have entered into the heart of man The things which God has prepared for those who love Him" (1 Cor. 2:9).

I further believe that heaven is a place as real as the place we are in now. Heaven is not a state of mind or a condition. If it were, God would have said, "Heaven is a state of mind, and when you go to your state of mind, this is what you can expect. . . ." It isn't necessary for all theologians to agree on exactly when and how the new heaven, the new earth, the new Jerusalem will finally be formed. God can be trusted to look after all of that.

The point is, we will live productively in a literal, perfect forever-place that is filled with the light and love of God. I do not believe we will be nebulous blobs. I've been a nebulous blob in this life, and when I get to heaven I expect to be a lot better than that! Some people think when we get to heaven we'll just be spirits floating around. Can you imagine? "Excuse me, I'm just an amoeba floating here. Have you seen Blob? Have you seen Nebe? Never mind, it doesn't really matter." The scripture teaches that we will have bodies fashioned like Jesus' glorified body. I believe we will recognize each other in heaven. I can recognize folks down here, and I don't expect to be any less intelligent in the world to come. God made us unique individuals and we will continue to be unique individuals when we leave this life, and "shall know just as I also am known" (1 Cor. 13:12).

What ages will the children be? Will my baby be a baby? Will he be full grown? Will God let me see him grow up? I don't know. . . "we see in a mirror dimly" (1 Cor. 13:12). We don't know all, but praise God we know enough to rejoice and take comfort.

I'm sure nobody ever passed through the gates of pearl with more delight and excitement than Cindy did. There is something significant to me about the twelve gates of heaven being made of pearl because pearls result from great struggle within the oyster shell. God causes the suffering to produce something beautiful rather than something ugly and horrible. Saints, passing through heaven's gates, have struggled and suffered, but God has finally said, "That's enough, come on up. Come on up to beauty and serenity."

The fellowship in heaven will be glorious, beyond description. Just think what it will be like to be enveloped in the love of millions of perfected Christians. . . . Christians who love completely, who are totally right with God. What an incredible outlook!

In order for us to enter heaven, of course we must exit this world. This exit we call death. Death holds a certain dread for all of us. According to Scripture, it is our last battle on this earth. Paul refers to death as "the last enemy." The testimony of many dying Christians gives evidence to the fact that they are being lifted, weightlessly, into indescribable beauty, radiance, peace, and into the presence of Jesus Himself. And Scripture teaches that God sends His angels to escort the redeemed into His presence. We read the account of how He sent angels for Lazarus in Luke 16:22. "So it was that the beggar died, and was carried by the angels to Abraham's bosom." One reason angels accompany us is to protect us. Satan will still be ripping and clawing to claim our souls for himself. But the angels will be right there to guard us and see us safely home.

Billy Graham, in his book *Angels—God's Secret Agents*, aptly describes what happens:

> Death is robbed of much of its terror for the true believer, but we still need God's protection as we take that last journey. At the moment of death the spirit departs from the body and moves through the atmosphere. But the Scripture teaches that the devil lurks there. He is "the prince of the power of the air" (Ephesians 2:2). . . . But Christ on Calvary cleared a road through Satan's kingdom . . . .The moment of death is Satan's final opportunity to attack the true believer; but God has sent His angels to guard us at that time . . . .The way to life is by the valley of death, but the road is marked with victory all the way.[1]

Maybe your grief will usher in for you a new aware-ness of God's plan for eternity. When we live for God, death is but a shifting into high gear and going on with the journey. Herman Melville said, "Life is a voyage that's homeward bound." Home is heaven. Home is where Jesus is. Home is where Cindy and the baby are. And that same perfect home awaits you and me.

Jordan C. Khan made this observation, "You will get to heaven by accepting Christ as Savior, but by accepting Christ as Lord and Savior you will bring heaven down to yourself."[2] I like that style of thinking. In the midst of our pain, whatever blow may have caused it, our looking to Jesus will bring His heavenly touch to help heal the wound. . . right now.

Chapter 19
The Way of Love

Love and grief run on parallel tracks. Grief is automatic when a person or thing we love becomes lost to us. At the same time, if we make sure we continue to love after loss, it will have a curative affect. God's wisdom in naming love as the first and second greatest commandments never ceases to amaze me. It is proven out in every dimension of life.

My sister Judy stayed with me for a few days following Cindy's burial. One evening she, Rodney, and I went out for dinner together, and at the table, Judy and I began to reminisce about our family and the good times we had as kids.

We shared a warm and loving mountain family whose roots were deep in the Nantahala Valley of North Carolina. My dad was a large, strong man, and I adored him. No matter what the circumstances when I was growing up, as long as he was somewhere nearby, I was not afraid. My mom was a tiny pepper pod of a woman, wonderfully outrageous in her gift for fun. She thought life ought to be a blast—and that is just what she made it for herself and everybody else. (I guess I must be like her.) My sister, Romana, was fourteen years older than I, so she watched after me a lot and became my second mom. Sonny, my brother, made my life miserable (just as big brothers are supposed to do). But I learned to admire him as he grew up to be one of the finest Christian men

I know. If friends were money, Sonny would be the wealthiest man around. Judy was beautiful, and she was solid like Dad. She became my encourager. I was the baby of the family, and they all loved and spoiled me in their own ways.

Two other people who greatly contributed to my young life were my Aunt Olive and my Uncle Emmett. They were down-to-earth mountain people like us, and I spent a lot of days and nights with them. Aunt Olive was a Christian to the tenth power. She always petted me, treated me special, and prayed for me with all her heart. Uncle Emmett used to take me fishing. He took pride in seeing me catch my first fish, a big native trout. And the last time I saw him before he died, he reminded me of that fishing trip and how my catch had been the envy of all the fishermen in "them parts." Uncle Emmett knew nothing about modern psychology, behavior modification, or the like, but he treated me as his own son, and his positive reinforcement strengthened my belief in myself.

At home we rarely sat down to a meal with just family present. Our home was a haven for family, friends, and sometimes strangers; and we were taught by example to love them all. As a result of this, I still like to be in a crowd, and I keep people around me most of the time. I like sharing my life, and anything I have, with other people. It's the only kind of life I've ever known—or would ever want to know.

Mom and Dad practiced before us the acceptance of people without judgment or criticism. I never heard my parents rip anybody; but when confronted with what appeared to be inappropriate behavior on someone's part, they always assumed the position that we do not walk in their shoes and we cannot know what they're feeling. They preferred to stretch out generous, loving hands rather than to judge.

In thinking about those who loved me, my thoughts naturally go back to Cindy. Cindy loved me, and God knows I loved her too. Together we loved our baby. My heart had been so bound to that arrangement, I wondered if losing them meant losing all love. But the truth is, when Cindy died, love did not end. Love kept on going because "God is love" (1 John 4:8). Many people showed boundless love toward me and toward the memory of Cindy in the days that followed our tragedy. I needed their love, and they still needed my love too. If I had closed down my will to love, I would have shut out the possibility of Robin's entrance into my life.

John Powell sheds light on the importance of love in these words from *Why Am I Afraid to Love?* "We are, each one of us, the product of those who have loved us—or refused to love us."[1] At least in part, I am who I am because of the force of love. Dr. Karl Menninger said that "love is the key to the entire therapeutic program of the modern psychiatric hospital." Perhaps love, after all, does make the world go around. Being loved is curative. But more than that, loving is curative too.

Several times I have seen television interviews with men or women who have been left all alone. In order to fill the void in their lives, they have reached out to help others. Some were caring for children with special needs, some were feeding the hungry, some were working with the elderly. But they all had in common the fact that they were meeting the needs of other people, and in so doing they were finding happiness and fulfillment for themselves. They were demonstrating love's action and reward. One precious lady was standing among little boys and girls with whom she was working. With a broad and toothy smile she boasted, "I'm loved and I'm hugged. I've cried with them, and they've cried with me." In my view that's living and loving!

Grief will test our caring about others because we tend to turn inward, concentrating on our own pain. We must guard against losing the ability to care about what other people are feeling and experiencing. Caring gives life its deepest significance. For years caring about Cindy had given meaning to my life. Paradoxically, the caring now ripped me apart. Yet my caring could be transferred to other people. There was much loving yet for me to do. . . and I thought, *Who knows, maybe it could be a road out of grief. After all, the Bible presents a relational theology. It says more about relationships than it does about anything else, and love is its theme.*

When you are in deep sadness, try, with the help of God, reaching down into yourself for the love that He has placed there, then reach out to touch someone who needs your love. It can give you a reason to go on.

You might protest that you just can't feel love because of the desolation that binds itself to you, and I can certainly identify with that. But liberation comes with our realization that love has little to do with feeling. Love is action—doing things that Jesus would do whether we feel like it or not.

The most supreme act of love the world has ever seen was the death of Jesus Christ, God incarnate, for sinful people. Do you think that as our Lord hung on a shameful, brutal cross, He was filled with warm and affectionate feelings for those who put Him there? I don't think so. It makes more sense that in His humanness He was feverishly dealing with his pain, His disappointment, and His rejection from both heaven and earth. But He permitted the cross to happen anyway.

Love goes beyond feelings when it seems we have no more strength to love and care. Love goes beyond tiredness when there's nothing left in us but exhaustion. Love goes beyond our own needs when others have needs. And love goes beyond human effort because God's Holy Spirit will show the love of Jesus through us.

You may find, as I did, that moments come in grief when there is a pause in the depression. . . brief moments of relief from the pain. Those pauses may occur as you catch a glimpse of the sunlight streaming through a morning window, or hear a word of reassurance, or some other simple thing. These hesitations offer you opportunities to determine anew to love the way Jesus loved and to generate acts of tenderness toward others. If you use these moments in such a positive way, you just might find that it will help you get through your suffering.

According to Henry Drummond, "To love abundantly is to live abundantly, and to love forever is to live forever. Hence, eternal life is inextricably bound up with love. . . .So long as [mankind] has friends, those who love him and whom he loves, he will live because to live is to love."[2]

Certainly I believe that Cindy is alive in a far better place than the one she left. I believe, too, that Cindy lives on in those of us who loved her. We like to talk about her and tell stories about things she said and did, and through the stories she lives among us. People who never even met her know her well. She lives on because she lives in our love.

Death does not have the final word.

Chapter 20

Pain—An Acceptable Guest

As individuals, we experience grief differently. Some people hold it in; some fight to get rid of it. No matter how we deal with grief, it is always painful. When we mourn a loss, we hurt. And the matter of getting on with our lives is attended to in the midst of pain.

I missed only one Sunday from my pulpit following Cindy's death. The next week I thought I should get back and prove out the faith I taught. . . the loving care of God when we hurt.

My parents came to hear me that Sunday. Cindy's parents came too. Everybody was there to support me and pick up the pieces if I fell apart. My sermon included the following comments:

> I am preaching this morning from the book of Job. Did you think I would preach from any other book? Job is known for his suffering, and in the scripture I'm going to read, he was at a difficult point in his life. He had reached a time when he didn't understand his circumstances. [My scripture reading included Job 23:10-11, 13 NAS.] "His hand is heavy. . . but He knows the way I take; When He has tried me, I shall come forth as gold. My foot has held fast to His path. . . . He is unique and who can turn Him? And what His soul desires, that He does.
>
> I cannot come to you saying I have all the

answers, or that because I have a loving relationship with my God everything is fine. That is far from the truth. There is deep hurt in my heart and I am struggling by the hour. But I can come to you saying there is also unexplainable joy in my heart because I know where Cindy and the baby are. As Vance Havner said, after his beloved wife went to be with the Lord, "Lost is not the right word for Christians divided by death. You haven't lost anything when you know where it is."

Remembering what I'd learned from Nelson Price concerning Cindy's being with one who loved her more than I did, I explained to my congregation:

> Christ died for Cindy while she was still a sinner. God said to me, "Ike, if you had seen all of the sinful side of Cindy, you wouldn't have lived with her, much less died for her. But I loved her completely. I loved the dark side of her, and I died for her." The hope we have in Christ puts death—and even the pain of death—in a proper perspective.

As I stood before those who loved Cindy and understood her fun-loving nature, as well as mine, my sense of humor surfaced:

> I know that God is going to take care of Cindy. He'll take better care of her than I did. And, man, that'll require some more care! I mean, after all, I did pretty well by her. I put her in a castle, gave her a nice car, and honestly, I dressed the girl like I made $200,000 a year. I'm sure heaven's charge account just went up, and the Lord only knows the cost of the robe she's already picked out!

All the time I was preaching I tried to keep in mind that there were others who were hurting too. I was not the only person who had a problem. Folks had come to the worship service to be uplifted. They needed nurturing, and they needed to be wisely instructed in the meaning of, "His hand is heavy. . . ." They needed to

understand that the heavy hand is guiding and protect-
ing, even when we feel that it is bearing down with a
pressure we can't endure. "Coming forth as gold" doesn't
interest us nearly as much as peace and comfort. We
would rather be left alone than to withstand the discom-
fort of refinement. I became aware of the holes in my own
faith when I read, "And what His soul desires, that He
does." You can say that again—we don't even get a vote.
In our humanness we try to avoid all pain—physical and
emotional—and as Christians, we become somewhat
ambivalent in our approach to the spiritual maturation
process. I was subject to wide mood swings regarding the
providence of God in my life, even though I believed He
"knows the way I take." I assured my people that in the
dark times, our feet can be "held fast to His path". . . even
though I didn't feel it half as loud as I said it.

In the evening service, I opened up a little more,
basing my remarks on Joseph Pieper's concept that the
two basic temptations in grief are presumption and
despair. "At times I have presumptuously taken things
into my own hands," I confessed. "I've been guilty of
telling God that I thought He blew it. I've nursed the idea
that, since Cindy and I were developing a Christian
home, He'd destroyed His own work." I confessed, too,
that falling into despair had been so easy. More than
once I had already said to myself, *I give up. Hey, I've lived
for God, and where'd it get me? God took everything I
cared about. Why shouldn't I just throw in the towel and
forget my commitment to Him? What's the use anyway?*

As you grieve, you may find presumption and despair tracking you too. The answer for you is the same as
it was for me: Jesus loves you, and Jesus is alive. That
sounds so simplistic when you're hurting, doesn't it? But
somehow, my belief in the resurrection kept pulling me
back to stability and hope. And if you keep it before you,
it will anchor you too. It's a historical fact that Jesus
lived on earth, died, and was resurrected. He did that
because He loves us; and if He loves us, He cares about
us, actively and sincerely. "The LORD is near to those
who have a broken heart" (Ps. 34:18).

At the time I was trying to recover from Cindy's

death, I was influenced more than a little by the television mindset of my generation. We grew up seeing things worked out in thirty minutes. No matter what the problem, it could be solved in an hour at the longest. The Cartwrights worked everything out in an hour, and "Father Knows Best" took only thirty minutes. Every day I told myself, *Today is the day I'm going to put things back together. Preachers are brave. They defend God. I can't ruin my reputation, and God's too, by failing now.*

Ministers of the gospel of Christ suffer a unique pain in grief. We are inclined to lay on ourselves the impossible responsibility of grieving perfectly. . . however we may interpret that. We want to set an example of total adequacy in pain, and in doing this we compound our suffering.

If you should ever find your pastor in bereavement of some nature, let me encourage you to keep his humanness in mind. To use a cliche: when preachers are cut, they bleed too. Dashed hopes and dreams devastate them and try their faith just as it does anyone else's. Not one of them is up to being a god for his parishioners.

In thinking of the pain of grief, I am compelled to mention the gnawing loneliness that we must go through. Someone has said that loneliness comes in only one size—extra large. I was intolerably lonely for Cindy. I couldn't expect anything else. John Milton said, "Loneliness is the first thing which God's eye nam'd not good." God did that just before He gave Adam a wife. The closeness of some relationships is so important to us, we're ripped apart when they end. There were days in my recovery I wished I had just stayed numb—the way I was the day Cindy died. Feeling nothing was better than feeling the racking pain that followed.

Are you undergoing lethal pain and loneliness? I won't offer you a platitude for that. Wounds heal slowly, and at times we must just be with the pain and wait for a pain-free day. What I can tell you is that the pain-free day will come. Though you may experience setbacks, little by little the open wound will close. In the book *How to Survive the Loss of a Love*, the authors give a helpful discussion of pain following loss. "Expect the pain when it comes, but don't dwell on it. Accept it, but don't invite it. Pain is an acceptable guest, but not a welcome long-term visitor."[1] I think this is a good way to think about it. It's okay to accept pain as normal and wait for relief. In grief, the pain stays with us for a long time. It is possible, however, for us to be clinging to it rather than the other way around. We need to make sure we are not deliberately coddling or holding on to our pain.

Overcoming loss is a process. Deep wounds are not healed overnight. Grief recovery requires patiently waiting for things to get better, remembering that God is in the waiting. Words from the Psalms and Isaiah helped me with this waiting.

> Wait on the LORD;
> Be of good courage,
> And He shall strengthen your heart;
> Wait, I say, on the LORD!
> >   Psalm 27:14

> But those who wait on the LORD
> Shall renew their strength;
> They shall mount up with wings like eagles
> They shall run and not be weary,
> They shall walk and not faint.
> >   Isaiah 40:31

I'm impressed with Frederick W. Faber's words, "We must wait for God, long, meekly, in the wind and wet, in the thunder and lightning, in the cold and the dark. Wait, and he will come. He never comes to those who do not wait." I think Faber must have known the pain of grief, don't you?

Chapter 21
Dealing with the Darkness

"I really don't know how to grieve," someone said to me recently. That was moment of truth, because those who are going through grief, especially for the first time, truly walk in darkness. As you grieve, it is important to remember there is no usual or acceptable way to do it. Do not expect to follow anybody else's blueprint or instructions, and don't feel guilty about the way you grieve even if well-meaning family and friends point out some "oughts" and "shoulds" that you happen not to be observing. I would like to rehearse here some things I learned about how we act and react during grief that may be of help to you.

It could be said that some of us grieve acutely, that is, the magnitude of pain is almost, if not altogether, debilitating in the early stages. Then, the acute griever moves on with the ability to put his or her life back together again. On the other hand, for some, the heavy pain may run a much longer course producing more of a chronic grief experience. In chronic grief, one endures the deep pain of loss over many months, perhaps years. There are other patterns, however, and it may be that you can't put yourself precisely in either category. We grieve according to personal variables, such as our psychological makeup and our circumstances.

Sometimes in grief we experience emotions that surprise us: agitation, fear, anxiety, hostility, a preoccupation without sadness, sleep disturbances, hopelessness, regret, guilt. We may feel we are shedding too many tears, and we may find ourselves weeping unexpectedly in what we consider an inappropriate (or at least inconvenient) time and place. These reactions are not uncommon. I know people who felt they were mentally ill because they were encountering emotions that were so foreign to them. Following the death of a loved one, some people experience a sense of the presence of the person lost, and even attest to seeing the absent loved one again.

As you work through jumbled emotions, you may find yourself moving back and forth from encouragement to dismay for quite some time. When you become more and more desensitized to the painful reminders you find in certain sights, sounds, and thoughts, you will begin to feel better. For example, the first Christmas following the loss of a special person is extremely painful, but as a conditioning process takes place, the pain decreases with subsequent Christmases.

It will be therapeutic for you to find a good shoulder to cry on. It may be a family member or a friend, but find someone with whom you are comfortable, someone with whom you can talk and cry without feeling ashamed or embarrassed. Express your emotions and listen to your own troubled feelings. Let others help you. Others who care are like "rods" and "staffs" comforting us when we walk the shadowy valley.

You may find that grief is putting a strain on some of your relationships. You need to be understood, and yet it may be impossible for those who have not traveled the road to understand. . . and no one really travels your road. At a time when you are having to accept an unwanted loss, it is difficult to accept a friend or family member's lack of understanding. But it will lighten your own burden if you will lower your expectations of others, and accept their limitations, as well as their condolences.

Although concentration may be difficult, reading is often good therapy. I don't know what I would have done without books written by those who had experienced grief and by others who have studied the effects of grief on individuals.

Without a doubt, the Word of God provides the greatest source of strength for troubled times. God made us and He knows us better than we know ourselves. Read the Bible and pray even when you feel empty and futile while you're doing it. Remember, God is not dependent on your feelings or your strength. I cannot give you a specific answer about how He will help you. But I can promise you, because He promises you, that your answers lie with Him. He will show you the way to walk, and He will give you strength and guidance to walk in that way.

In a time of grief, you may feel an unrelenting anger that you had not expected. Anger is a passion that nearly always finds its way into our feelings to some degree when something has been taken from us against our will. As odd as it seems, we may feel anger at the one who died. Robin recalls feeling extremely angry with Phil for getting killed and leaving her to pick up the pieces of a shattered life. I, too, remember feeling angry because I was the one left to find a way to carry on. If unresolved problems, incomplete plans, or unmet expenses are left to be dealt with, it could add to the anger felt by the one who survives.

When tragedy hit my life, I got angry with God. I went through only a day or so of that, though, because a day or so was about all I could take. I vented all of my frustrations and all of my hurts. Then when I got through, I felt God speaking right to me, "Are you through?" And I said, "Yes, I'm through." Then, some healing started to take place. Anger is normal, no matter the direction we aim it, and we need not feel guilty when we experience hostility or resentment in grief.

Extreme sadness is to be expected and is not considered clinical depression. But if you lose all interest in life, if you come to the point where you cannot function, and these symptoms continue over a long period of time, you may be chemically depressed. A chemical depression is, simply put, a biochemical depletion in body chemistry; and it can be induced by prolonged stress.[1] Should you reach this state, you need to get help from someone who understands depression. In my story I have described my emotional downward spiral which did, in fact, lead to depression. I put myself in a double bind, denying my feelings, trying to outrun my sadness and confusion only to wind up in a depressed state that I could not handle alone. I suffered some of depression's typical manifestations such as panic disorders, heart palpitations, and the feeling of being in a black hole I couldn't climb out of. Certainly this type of depression does not happen to everyone who grieves. It may not happen to you, but if it does, remember much can be done to speed your recovery.

Whenever depression occurs, professional help is urgently needed. Keep in mind there are good, Christian, mental health professionals who are assisting Christians every day. Should you have difficulty finding one, check with your church or a church in your area. Many churches, especially the larger ones, provide counseling services. If yours does not, your pastor or some other local pastor will probably have a good reference list of Christian counselors who can help you recover emotionally and learn a healthy way to think and live.

I could not speak about depression if I did not take the opportunity to make it clear that Christians are not exempt from depression. Great faith is not always the only answer to depression-free living. The prevailing notion that a Christian who is exercising faith cannot become depressed is one of Satan's most devastating lies. Pastor Maxie Dunnam, in an article in *Preaching* magazine has spoken to this misconception in an excellent way: "One of the problems with Christians is that we think there is something wrong with our Christian experience if we admit that we're not on top. . . . I think this shows how powerful the devil is: causing masses of Christians to adopt a model that even Jesus didn't fit." When I read this thought about Gethsemane and our Savior's bloody sweat and despondent plea, "Let this cup pass," and I thought about the pathetic cry from the cross, "My God, my God, why hast thou forsaken me?" I realized that depression is not confined to the faithless.

The psalmist cried,

> O My God, I cry in the daytime, but You do not
>   hear;
> And in the night season, and am not silent. . . .
>
> I am poured out like water,
>   And all My bones are out of joint;
> My heart is like wax;
>   It has melted within Me.
> My strength is dried up like a potsherd,
>   And My tongue clings to My jaws;
> You have brought Me to the dust of death"
>   (Ps. 22:2, 14, 15).

Was this psalmist depressed or what?

Yet the sound of true praise rings out as this chapter moves on:

> My praise shall be of You in the great
>   congregation;. . .
> Those who seek Him will praise the LORD"
>   (Ps. 22:25, 26).

And after this psalm the glorious twenty-third flows in with its infinite peace, "The LORD is my shepherd; I shall not want. . . ."

The psalmist knew God was the answer to his depression. He knew that in God could be found the answers to all of his darkness and pain. He swung far out in depression, but every time he did, he acknowledged the goodness of God and swung back toward his Creator and the sure hope He provided. And here's a flash for us: Nothing has changed. "Jesus Christ is the same yesterday, today, and forever" (Heb. 13:8). God in Christ supplies our needs even when we are depressed. Though our voices may crack when we praise, our throats may ache when we pray, and our steps may falter with spasmodic faith, He is faithful. Our trusting may seem absurd to the world, and even to us, but the object of our trust will reward us in due time.

Chapter 22

Bitter or Better

I heard a wonderful story about a man who was seated on a park bench when a little guy about five years old sauntered up and sat down beside him. The little boy started winding what appeared to be a prized possession—a dollar watch. "My, what a pretty watch," The man remarked. "Does it tell you the time?"

"No, sir," replied the little fellow. "You gotta look at it."

Jesus Christ is available to help us in our distresses, but we "gotta look at" Him. We can hear how He helped others, we can read the testimonies of spiritual applications others have made from now until He comes again, but if we do not look at Him for ourselves, we affect nothing in our own experience.

Job 5:7 says, "Man is born to trouble, As the sparks fly upward." As surely as we have life, we have trouble and sorrow. As long as we live, we will have occasions for mourning. In these times we ultimately come to the point of choice as to how we deal with our situation. We decide whether we will make Jesus Christ our friend or our enemy. I've seen people in grief reach this crossroad at different points in time depending on personality and situation. But they always reach a point of decision. . . they always make a choice to get bitter or better.

The matter is settled in our faith. How is it with you? Have you reached the place where you must choose to

rule the situation or let it rule you? Does your faith grant
God permission to allow things to happen that you do not
agree with? Does your faith make room for loving and
believing God when things happen that deeply disappoint and hurt you? Is God sovereign in your life after
all? When everything is said and done, grief, like all of
life's difficulties calls on us to believe God even when we
are unexplainably wounded. When we don't understand
the whys of our circumstances, but continue in a good
spirit anyway, we are exercising our faith—the purest
form of worship. If we understood, there would be no
need for faith. If the answer were always "yes," there
would be no need for prayer.

In struggle, most of us learn about true faith for the
first time. We come to know in reality for the first time.
We come to know in reality what it is to "walk by faith,
not by sight" (2 Cor. 5:7). Our faith is precious to God;
nothing pleases Him more. Hebrews 11:6 tells us, "without faith it is impossible to please Him." And Jesus
asked, "when the Son of Man comes, will He really find
faith on the earth?" (Luke 18:8). Faith is the foundation
of the Christian life. A childlike faith is the key to
salvation, the key to Christian living, and it is the key to
overcoming grief. Again, I do not mean to give a simplistic, pat answer—and, believe me, when people said, "just
have faith" to me after Cindy died, I rebelled. But I came
to understand it later on, and you will too if you choose
to.

Life is a warfare, and grief is one of its supreme
battles. We all fight giant problems in our lives. In 1
Samuel 17:9, Goliath roared to God's army to bring him
a man to fight: "If he is able to fight with me and kill me,
then we will be your servants. But if I prevail against
him and kill him, then you shall be our servants and
serve us." That is what the grief giant says to us: "Either
you beat me and I'll serve you, or I'll beat you and you'll
serve me." Each of us, allied with God, is all the army
needed to defeat the giant of grief.

Yes, there comes a time in grief when you will have
to take a stand and fight. It is a volitional act of the
determinant will. You grab your mental bootstraps and

pull. You choose to do the things that will promote your healing and wholeness. It will mean going out with friends when you'd rather not make the effort. It will mean rearranging your schedule to provide time for a hobby or a new interest. It will mean returning to church, perhaps alone, and finding a different pew in which to worship. Each one of us must choose the things that will help, and we often do it without the "good feeling" that we hope will follow later on.

It would be wonderful if, like when things got tough in Oz, we could just click our heels three times, grab Toto, and head for Kansas. But it only works that way "over the rainbow." In real life, recovery from sorrow entails a laborious effort. We can't wait until we are happy again to start the trying that places us on the road to recovery. We simply must get at it, and when we do, we usually find that action produces motivation.

We make a step in faith. We take up the battle in the strength of the One who claimed that He overcame the world, the One who sits at the right hand of God and does battle for us in ways we cannot understand, the One who enables us to sing the songs of victory.

> Encamped along the hills of light,
> Ye Christian soldiers, rise,
> And press the battle ere the night
> Shall veil the glowing skies.
> Against the foe in vales below
> Let all our strength be hurled;
> Faith is the victory, we know
> That overcomes the world.
> From "Faith is the Victory"
> By John H. Yates[1]

Never is our belief in God's care and protection more urgent than when we are suffering and can't feel His strength. The psalmist said, "He is our help and our shield" (33:20). It is significant that he does not say the Lord *provides* our help and shield. Rather he says He *is* our refuge and shield. God is our protector, our champion in the battle. We place our trust in the person of

Almighty God and lean on Him for victory.

A. W. Thorold said, "The highest pinnacle of the spiritual life is not joy in unbroken sunshine, but absolute and undoubting trust in the love of God." We go forth in the conflict "by faith and not by sight,". . . and certainly not by feeling.

We honor God in the highest way when we trust through pain, when we simply believe Him for triumph over the present and for the promise of a better day tomorrow.

In the book, *Restoring Your Spiritual Passion*, Gordon MacDonald told about walking with his wife through a neighborhood looking at the different types of architecture. Along the way they noticed a poster in one of the windows. The poster featured the silhouette of an open hand. It was positioned in a prominent place where even a child couldn't miss it. "That poster is a sign of a safe place," his wife told him. The poster was a sign to those who needed help that this was a home offering protection or assistance. If a person knocked on the door, he or she would be welcomed in and provided safety.[2]

God holds us in the safety of His nail-scarred hands. Someone has said that His hands are cupped because to close them would give us no freedom, and to hold them completely open would give us too little security. We are fastened to His hand by His unchanging nature and the blood of His Son. He holds us just right for our development and our safety. And He holds us forever.

Chapter 23

A Sovereign Strategy

Soren Kierkegaard said something to the effect that we live our lives forward, but we understand them backward. I feel the truth of Kierkegaard's observation when I look back at the events of my life. Charles Spurgeon's statement, which I mentioned earlier, is framed and sits on my desk for my frequent inspiration:

> God is. . .
> Too good to be unkind. . .
> Too wise to be mistaken. . .
> When you cannot trace His hand,
> You can always trust His heart.
>   Charles Spurgeon

In His infinite foreknowledge, God knew that I would come to love Him, so He began to prepare me to live out that love before I ever knew who He was. His hand guided, influenced, and led, long before I knew it was His hand.

I know now why God placed me in a wonderful, upbeat family. And I can see that his special gift to me was an incredible capacity for fun and happiness, a technicolor outlook, and a strong sense of future. The retrospect builds my faith in the Almighty's hand. I understand why God took me, a child safe in the rural mountains, and planted me in a big and unfamiliar city where I was different and insecure. I needed to learn the lessons that it taught.

His hand remained firmly on my life when I struggled in the inner city. . . through boyhood, through the teen years, and into young adulthood. In that setting I learned one of the most important lessons God taught me—that there is a struggle.

I was divinely protected when I ran with the tough crowd, went to jail, flunked out of college, and played at being a Christian. When my heart was far from Him, He sent me a wife who would demonstrate His love. Through her influence, and that of others who touched my life, I finally came to recognize the holy hand. When the going was rough, God gave me new hope at New Hope Baptist Church. . . where I found a home and a ministry among choice people of His family.

The mighty hand of God held me when grief inflicted its most profound cruelty. He traveled before me on the path of tears and gave me a faith that looks through death and sees a larger life beyond the grave. He taught me that it is not death to die!

The gift of Robin, Abigail, and Danielle was a restoration greater than I could have imagined. So I thank God for His strategy in my life. I praise Him for bringing me to where I am, and for continuing to guide me and contour me for His will.

I am telling my story, not for its uniqueness, but rather because it is ordinary—ordinary because God is moving in the lives of us all. And we can trust His judgments and rest in His care. The alterations in our lives are not just idle changes or disturbing interruptions. The events, though sometimes unexpected and unwanted, are meant to navigate our course and keep us ever walking with the Savior Jesus, "who dared to call His burden light."

In *A Grief Observed*, C. S. Lewis writes after losing his wife, "God has not been trying an experiment on my faith or love in order to find out their quality. He knew it already. It was I who didn't."[1] How splendidly God helps us learn about ourselves. How urgently we need to learn. Perhaps the simplest and surest thing we discover about living is that it's hard.

"Into each life some rain must fall" is a profundity attributed to Henry Wadsworth Longfellow. Snoopy, of *Peanuts* fame, must have had this thought in mind when, lying face up atop his house in the middle of a rainstorm, he muttered, "It rains on the just and the unjust, and right now it's raining in my face." Without question, the wind and rain of personal storm will fall in our faces. Few people escape the pain of losing loved ones, and that is not the only rain we encounter. The raindrops of life are as countless as the grains of sand on a crescent beach. And the overwhelming reality is that they will surely fall.

A. W. Tozer said, "It is doubtful whether God can bless a man greatly until He has hurt him deeply." It's difficult for me to think of God hurting a man. Still, it is obvious that He permits the hurts. Sometimes in our pain or after it, He opens the veil a little and lets us see purpose in what He has allowed.

For example, my loss has made me a much more sympathetic minister. When I enter a home or a hospital room where there is death or dying, I now enter as one who can share the feelings of those who are enduring the loss. I know the sorrow inflicted by the death of someone you love. I know because I've been there.

When I counsel with a depressed, anxious, or angry person, I'm more understanding than I used to be. I try to make allowances for what they're dealing with. Then, too, I'm more resourceful—better able to help—because I had to search for answers when I was depressed.

Because of my struggles I've moved a little closer to becoming the man God wants me to be. I see more clearly that God's strength in us is born out of our weakness. And I'm more aware that He wants to thrust me out where one person touches another in the tangled thickets of a hurting world. It was in my suffering that I received an increased capacity for loving those who are important to me and a deeper appreciation for each day that I have them with me. Perhaps these are the rewards Tozer was talking about when he said God could bless a man who had been deeply hurt.

Our major fear as Christians may be that when heartbreak comes, we won't cope the way we should. We try to borrow tomorrow's grace for today's needs, and we find it doesn't work that way. But my testimony is that when the crisis comes to us, the Christ of every crisis also comes.

I'm no different from any other Christian in that I want my life to be strong and victorious. I want to do it right. I want to please God. The only way I know how to accomplish this is to believe that He will be there with what I need when I need it. I try to trust Him, then leap out in faith and live, knowing that I do not fling myself out into darkness, but into the loving arms of a Father who takes pleasure in giving me strength for the day and bright hope for the future.

I applaud John Powell's assertion in *Fully Human, Fully Alive* when he says "I am sure that the most persistent and restless desire of my life is to be fully human and fully alive. . . . My personal prayers vary according to the experience and needs of the day, but one prayer is never omitted: 'O God, my Father, don't let me die without having really lived and really loved.'" And he goes on to quote Saint Irenaeus, "The glory of God is a human being who is fully alive!"[2]

Martin Luther is reported to have said, "Love God and sin boldly." Christian scholars have had a great time with that down through the years! I'm sure we'll never know all Luther had in his heart when he made that statement, but history shows us one thing for sure: Martin Luther jumped on life with both feet. He boldly took on the tasks as he saw them to be right and correct, and he trusted God to cover the rest. We would do well to imitate Luther's boldness for living.

In *The Shoes of the Fisherman*, Morris L. West offers a peerless commentary on life: "It costs so much to be a full human being that there are very few who have the enlightenment or the courage to pay the price. One has to abandon altogether the search for security and reach out to the risk of living with both arms. One has to embrace the world like a lover. One has to accept pain as a condition of existence. One has to court doubt and darkness as the cost of knowing. One needs a will stubborn in conflict, but apt always to total acceptance of living and dying." *God, help me to see that. There is no growin' without tough goin'.*

The day Cindy died and I found her snowflake necklace on the floor of the hospital room, I didn't understand what had happened to it. I held it out to Rodney. "What's wrong with this, Rodney?"

"It's lost its sparkle." He could see it too.

I handed it to Al Holley. "Look, Al. What's wrong with this necklace?" Al saw the same thing Rodney and I had seen. "It doesn't sparkle any more."

I tried to clean it with everything I could find, but nothing helped. I took it to a jeweler to have the diamonds mounted into a ring. When I asked him if he could make the diamonds shine again, he guaranteed me that he could.

Two weeks later I returned to pick up the ring. My jeweler friend met me in the parking lot, proudly exhibiting a beautiful, sparkling ring. "These stones are brilliant!" I exclaimed. "I don't understand it. What was wrong with them?"

"Do you really want to know?"

I assured the jeweler I did, and he gave an amazing explanation. "The thing that made the necklace lose its sparkle was Cindy's blood. Her blood had seeped into the setting and robbed the stones of their luster. I was able to clean it because, as a master jeweler, I knew what to do."

I decided to wear the ring all the time to remind me of the supreme Master Jeweler, Jesus Christ. Through His cleansing power, He gives light and life to my existence. And when human circumstances dulled my life, the Master gave it sparkle once again.

He did that for me. He can do it for you.

Introduction
to the Workbook

This workbook section contains additional insights and many reflection questions to help you think, pray, plan, and assimilate the concepts. In other words, it is designed to help you grieve.

You may want to go through this material alone. Take your time and pace yourself. The goal is not to fill in the blanks. The goal is to experience the Lord's healing touch as you express your hurt, pain, and confusion. Even if you do the workbook individually, share your responses with a trusted friend, pastor, or counselor so this person can give you comfort and feedback.

Many churches have grief support groups which use this book. In this affirming and powerful environment, you will learn from one another and feel the encouragement of this body of believers. The format of some groups takes people through the material for 12 or 13 weeks. If your group chooses to use this workbook in this way, you will probably start over again for the next quarter. You certainly won't be through grieving in three months! Other groups are ongoing and take a month or longer on each step. Either way can work well if people have realistic expectations.

I trust God will use this workbook to enlighten the eyes of your heart at the same time that He warms it.

Step 1
Embracing the Loss

That person you love is never going to be there again to give you a smile, a hug, or a word of love. That hurts so much. It's no wonder we want to avoid facing our pain. Some of us try to avoid facing it for years and years, but the more we run from it, the more it haunts and controls us.

One of the things that helped me break through the denial that Cindy was dead was the fact that I was right there with her in that operating room when she died. Only minutes before, I had walked out of her room. I had kissed her seven times, and we had kidded each other about whether it would be a boy or a girl. It was a precious time together. We gave each other thumbs up, and she said, "Go tell everybody I'm doing great!" And I walked out to give the good news that our baby would be delivered within the next two hours.

A few minutes later, I was in the hallway of that hospital walking back to Cindy's room when I heard on the intercom: "Ward 100." I don't have premonitions, but somehow I knew something was wrong with Cindy. I ran down the hallway to her room. With my own eyes, I saw those medical professionals do everything in their power to help her live. An incredible feeling swept through me . . . a feeling I hope to God I never feel again, like ice water through my body. In the middle of that awful time, I just closed my eyes and thought, "I can will this not to happen. I can will Cindy to get well." But when I opened my eyes, the doctors turned to me. I could tell by the look in their eyes that Cindy was gone. There was still one doctor pounding on Cindy's chest trying to revive her. I said to him, "Please, stop beating on her." He stopped and turned to me. I remember the pained look on his face when he said softly, "Yes, sir."

We walked out in the hallway. The doctors told me they weren't sure what happened. There was no panic. Only shock. After a few minutes, I went back in the room to find Cindy's necklace I'd given her. It meant so much to both of us. I looked all over, and I finally found it over in a corner. Somebody had ripped it off her to get it out of the way. I picked it up and walked over to Cindy. I pulled back the sheet covering her, and I looked at her lying there. I prayed, "God, even now I know You can raise her up. Just like Lazarus. God, please, please, raise Cindy back up! If You'll just let her live, I'll spend the rest of my life telling people how wonderful You are." I was bargaining with God.

But God didn't buy.

I squeezed her hand. . . hoping. . . hoping to feel her squeeze mine.

Nothing.

I laid down across her, and I kissed her lips.

Nothing.

Just an hour ago, my precious Cindy and I had been so happy together. Now there was nothing. Now I knew this was real. Cindy was dead. The first great stab of reality penetrated my soul.

I walked down the hall, and the doctors and other medical personnel said quietly, "People in the waiting room know something's wrong. We have to go tell them. Do you want us to do it?"

"No," I said. "I'll do it."

Family and friends were there to celebrate our child's birth. Now I had to take them much different news. I walked down the hall and opened the doors. I'll remember Cindy's mother's voice the rest of my life. She took one look at me and moaned, "Oh, no! Not my baby! Oh, no! Not my baby!" I knelt down and hugged her. I said, "I'm so sorry. We've lost her. Cindy's dead."

That moment just about killed me. It was the first time I said the words, "Cindy's dead."

A good friend drove me home that first night, but I hoped we wouldn't ever get there. Because Cindy wouldn't be there. It was empty. So empty.

I went to the funeral home to pick out a casket, and they asked me what she was going to wear. That was so hard.

To this day, I hate walking in hospitals. I don't like going to funeral homes. I don't even like the smell of masses of flowers or the cold touch of steel.

We left the baby with her. That's the way it was supposed to be. At the funeral, I held on to a pastor on our staff, Dr. Harry Smith. Harry was in his 80's, but I held on to him like he was an old oak tree. He had seen a lot of heartaches in his life, and he had come through strong. I thought that if I got close enough to him, maybe some of that would rub off on me. As we walked out, I remember the muffled shuffle of feet. I remember that sound.

I closed the door to the hearse. It was a heavy door, and it made a heavy, air-tight sound. Years later, I realized why I get anxious every time I hear the sound of the plane's door closing when I fly. It's the same sound as that hearse door when I shut the door on Cindy.

At the cemetery, I heard shoes crunch on the gravel. And I heard people crying.

Memories flooded my mind. I'll never forget her red hair. She was a baton twirler, a flirt, a laugh a minute. She loved life and loved people. She was so committed to God—much more than me. She really embraced life. That's what made it so hard.

To grieve is to embrace someone and to let them go at the same time. We can't depend on them like we did before. We have to let them go so we can move into the future. But we never, never forget them.

If we don't let them go, we run the risk of turning them into saints or idols to worship. We can create false images that the person was perfect. . . or perfectly horrible. We create an image that nobody alive can ever live up to.

We are identified closely with that person. In many relationships, we become an extension of each other—until death. At that moment, part of us dies and never comes back, but the result of grieving is a deeper, stronger life. Like the grain of wheat that must die and be sown in order to bring life, we must allow that part of us to die so we can have new life, too.

If we refuse to grieve, our heart aches continually. We live in the past, hoping it will change, knowing it won't. Nothing in that past can give fuel for tomorrow. We get bogged down in hurt, anger, and a million "what if's." We think the best part of our lives is over, and that robs us of hope for the future. Sure, grieving is one of the hardest things we'll ever have to do, but we pay a high emotional price for refusing to grieve.

Temperaments and Grief

You may recall a paragraph in the first chapter which described four different temperament types and how they typically handle grief. These four are:

● People who are outgoing and optimistic often get very busy. They try to fill up their lives with people and things to do so they won't have to feel the pain.

● Reflective people often withdraw into a shell and become very pensive and sad. They think and feel deeply about the loss, and usually need some encouragement to get out and get going again.

● People who are organized and detailed often think they could have done "just one more thing" and prevented the death. They believe, "I should have seen this coming. I should have planned better." They are often consumed with guilt for not doing enough, even though they did all that could possibly be done for that person.

● The tough, decisive people just get angry—at the person for dying, at the doctors and nurses for not doing enough, at other family members for crying so much, and at themselves (though they may not admit it) for feeling so helpless.

❑ Which of these (or what combination of these) best characterizes you and your grief experience so far? Explain:

❑ List each member of your family and close friends. Which of the temperament types (or combination of them) best characterizes each of them?

❑ Does identifying their "grief temperament" help you be more patient and understanding with them? Why or why not?

Avoiding Pain

We can try to avoid the pain of our loss by:

● Denying the significance of it, such as saying, "She wasn't the mother I needed anyway. I don't miss her."

● Minimizing the hurt: "It's not that bad. I'm over it now anyway."

● Pretending the person never existed: Refusing to think about, talk about, or look at anything that could remind you of that person.

● Isolating: Staying away from anybody and everybody who might talk about the deceased person.

● Refusing to go through the deceased's effects: Leaving

the desk, room, clothes, and other things the way they were when the person died.

● Blaming: Instead of feeling the hurt, we express outrage at those who failed to keep our loved one alive or provide the care and comfort we perceived that person deserved. We may blame doctors, nurses, family members, friends... or ourselves. Our anger, then, is a lid to keep us from delving into our hurt.

● Idolizing: We make that person into "the perfect father" or "perfect mother" or husband or child or whatever. This keeps us from facing the reality that the person wasn't the Prince or Princess Charming we secretly hoped, and therefore, we not only need to grieve that person's death, we also need to grieve the loss of our dream that this person would meet all our needs, hopes, and desires.

❑ Are any of these a part of your grief experience? If so, which one(s)? Explain:

Love/Loss History

Our lives contain many high points and low points. It is often helpful to stop and reflect on those times in our lives when we felt particularly loved, and those times when we experienced loss. Keep in mind, there are many different kinds of losses we experience, not just death. We feel the pangs of loss when:
● an engagement is broken off
● a child leaves home
● we move away from friends
● we are fired or don't get promoted as we hoped
● we feel betrayed by a friend
● ongoing losses like living with an alcoholic parent or spouse, or experiencing abuse or neglect
● divorce

- chronic or acute disease
- severe injury
- and many other instances in our lives.

A Love/Loss History gives you the opportunity to chart the significant events in your life and how you responded to them. On the left, list those events or periods of your life in which you felt particularly loved, strong, and secure. On the right, list your losses. For instance, a man named Jim recorded:

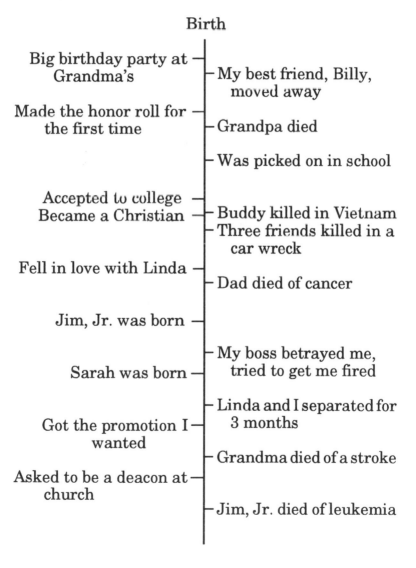

Birth

Big birthday party at Grandma's — — My best friend, Billy, moved away

Made the honor roll for the first time — — Grandpa died

— Was picked on in school

Accepted to college — Became a Christian — — Buddy killed in Vietnam — Three friends killed in a car wreck

Fell in love with Linda — — Dad died of cancer

Jim, Jr. was born —

— My boss betrayed me, Sarah was born — tried to get me fired

— Linda and I separated for Got the promotion I — 3 months wanted

— Grandma died of a stroke

Asked to be a deacon at — church

— Jim, Jr. died of leukemia

❑ Take a few minutes to stop, get quiet, pray and reflect. As you chart your Love/Loss History, you may think of events and people (both positive and negative, pleasant and painful) you haven't thought of in years, and you may think of relatively minor events in your life. If you think of them during this time, it may indicate they are more important than you previously thought.

Birth

❑ Now, list each positive event or loving, supportive person on the left of your chart. For each one, describe how that love or that success made you feel and act at that time.

❑ Are there any patterns in your loves and successes? Explain:

❑ Are there any patterns in how you responded to these loves and successes? Explain:

❑ List each painful person or negative event on the right and describe how that loss made you feel and act at that time.

❑ Were there any ongoing losses, such as abuse, neglect, or living with an alcoholic parent or spouse? If so, list and describe these here:

❑ How did these ongoing losses shape your life (motivations, hopes, fears, health, etc.)?

❑ Are there patterns in the types of losses, the intensity of them, or the timing of them? Explain:

❑ Describe the pattern of your responses to these losses:

❑ Which of these losses are "complete," that is, you have grieved them and the "dagger of hurt" has been removed?

❑ Which of the losses still causes you to feel deep pangs of hurt, to cry, or to withdraw?

❑ What have you learned about yourself and your typical grief responses by doing this Love/Loss History?

Relating to God

In several places in this book, I have described how I sometimes felt very close to God during the weeks and months after Cindy died, but sometimes felt very distant from Him.

❑ Read each of these three passages of Scripture several times. Try to feel what the writers were feeling when they penned the words. Then write a brief summary or paraphrase of each one.

Psalm 13:1-4:

Psalm 73:21-26

Psalm 23

❑ Which of these passages best describes your experience with God right now? Explain:

❑ Write a prayer to the Father honestly expressing your feelings, fears and hopes.

Heavenly Father, I'm feeling. . .

I'm afraid. . .

Lord, I hope. . .

Find a Friend

I hope you're not trying to go through your grieving alone. That is so painful and so hard. Maybe you're in a grief support group, or maybe you are spending time with your pastor or a counselor. Or maybe you have a dear friend or family member who is walking this path by your side. If you don't have someone, please take the initiative this week to call your pastor, a counselor, or a hospital in your area so you can find a person or a group. That is vitally important to help you go—and grow— through this dark time.

Step 2
Myths, Stupid Things, and Plans

We pick up perspectives about loss and grief from our families and friends, from books and articles, and from our churches. Some of these perspectives are good and healthy, but many of them are erroneous. They are myths masquerading as truth. If we believe these myths, we probably will be hurt even worse, and we won't have the insight and encouragement to grieve appropriately. Let's look at some of these myths:

● Time heals all wounds.

No it doesn't. Anybody who tells you that time heals all wounds either has never been deeply wounded or hasn't learned what grief is about. The passing of time doesn't heal anything at all, unless we use that time to grow in our awareness, take responsibility, and take the actions we need to take.

● You've just got to get back to the business of living.

My friend, if you haven't taken care of the business of the dying, you won't be prepared to truly live again. You have to come to grips with the significance of the loss in the present before you can be free to embrace the future.

● Keep busy.

Living in a flurry of activity can help dull the pain . . . temporarily. But what happens when you lay down to go to sleep? All the feelings of loss are then compounded by the fear of facing that loss, and nighttime can be a horror. Keeping busy can take your mind off things, and certainly, we need to take care of whatever we are responsible to do, but using activity to cover our pain only makes it worse.

● You can will yourself to get over the pain.

A lady who felt the deep pangs of losing her husband was told by a man in her church, "You just need to pull yourself up by your bootstraps and get over it."

She looked at him in the eye and said, "Some days, I can't find my bootstraps. In fact, some days I can't even find my boots."

When we try to will the pain away, we may deaden it for a while, but the wound resurfaces in some way. Some people who suppress the hurt and anger become like volcanoes, smouldering for a while, then exploding in the hot lava of rage. Others develop psychosomatic illnesses because their bodies can't cope with the stress of denial. And still other people become deeply depressed. Don't try to will the hurt to go away and pretend it isn't there. Admit it. Feel it. Grieve it.

● Talking about your pain only makes it worse.

Talking to a trusted friend can bring those repressed feelings to the surface so you can be aware of them and honest about them, but that doesn't make them worse. Those feelings of hurt, anger, fear, resentment, sadness, confusion, and a myriad of other emotions are the normal baggage of loss. Denying them only makes them fester, and it makes it more difficult to deal with them later.

● You have to grieve alone.

Well, it's true that nobody can grieve for you, but the truth is, no one can grieve effectively alone. We all need someone to lean on, someone to understand us, someone who will listen and not fix us. And we need that person to gently point us toward wholeness and healthy actions so we don't get bogged down in a pity party. Our supportive friends may not feel exactly the way we do, but they care. God made us relational beings. We need each other.

● Just replace the loss.

I know a boy whose dog was run over by a truck. That boy loved that old dog, and he cried and cried. The boy's grandfather tried to console him by saying, "Don't cry. I'll get you another dog this weekend." The boy didn't feel comforted at all. He didn't want a new dog. He wanted the one that was lying in the street. The old man thought he was helping, but his offer was an attempt to bypass the boy's real grief.

Sometimes people will tell us to replace the loss of a loved one, too. Only days (I'm not kidding. This is the truth.) after Cindy died, I had people calling me offering to line me up with dates! They were well-meaning, but so misguided. We can never replace someone we love. We can grieve, and we can move on, but that person can never be replaced.

● Anger is sin.

Some of us Christians are so uncomfortable with anger, and for good reason in many cases. We may have seen a parent or a spouse's violent outbursts, or we may have grown up in a home where any demonstration of anger was strictly forbidden. When we get angry about our loss now, we feel guilty, unclean, ashamed. The feeling of anger isn't sin. Paul told us in Ephesians to "be angry." Now is the time to follow that command! But Paul also says, "but do not sin." So there's a limit. Don't let your feelings of anger propel you to angry behaviors like taking revenge, withdrawing, or hurting others in some way. Let the emotion be a signal that your loss may be deeper than you thought. Underneath most anger is more hurt. If your anger is explosive or persistent, ask yourself, "What deeper hurt lies under that anger?" That will be a productive response to your anger.

● If you let yourself feel, you'll be overwhelmed (or you're a wimp).

Some of us are so uncomfortable with our emotions that we are afraid we will pass some "point of no return" if we allow ourselves to cry and express how we really feel. That's why it's so important to have a partner, a friend who will walk that valley with us. I'll be honest, there were plenty of times I felt overwhelmed. . . but I made it through. You will, too. It takes courage to feel those awful feelings. Don't try to do it alone.

Most men take a little different track. They refuse to

feel because it isn't macho. They don't want to be wimps, so they won't let themselves feel the pain. They feel okay about expressing anger, so they blame anybody and everybody for the death or for not caring enough in the last hours. But this anger is a covering for their deep hurts.

● Don't get close to anyone again. It hurts too much to lose them.

Sure, it hurts to lose someone, but remember the old saying, "Better to have loved and lost than never to have loved at all." That saying is usually used in connection with dating and love, but it applies here very well, too. Life is ultimately about two things: relationships and risks. And those two go hand-in-hand. If we try to avoid any risks of being hurt again, we will miss out on the love and meaning that God intends for all of us. Some of us now believe, "If I don't love, I won't get hurt." But the hurt that comes from an empty life is far worse than loving and losing again.

● "Joy comes in the morning."

I've actually heard a few people who experienced the death of a child or a spouse say, "I got up the next morning, and I was praising God that I was over the hurt!" I have one thing to say about that, and my comment comes from years of deep theological study and the study of human behavior: Baloney!

A few people quoted me that verse (Psalm 30:5) when I was in the depths of grieving over Cindy. They wanted to be helpful, and I sure wanted to believe them, but my grieving took a little longer than that! Counselors who work with those who grieve say that it takes at least two years to grieve a death, perhaps four years if the death was sudden or suicide, and even longer if it resulted from a criminal act. Certainly God is real during that time, and the morning comes eventually, but expectations of quick and painless grief only compound the hurts.

● Memories will always be painful.

In the days after we lose one we love, almost all memories are painful because they rub the open wound of our loss. But over time, we will enjoy the memories we shared together. We'll enjoy telling stories, and we'll laugh again. That, too, is a part of the grief process.

❏ To what extent have you believed each of these myths? Indicate them on a scale of 0 (not at all) to 10 (hook, line and sinker!):

—Time heals all wounds.

0   1   2   3   4   5   6   7   8   9   10

—You've just got to get back to the business of living.

0   1   2   3   4   5   6   7   8   9   10

—Keep busy.

0   1   2   3   4   5   6   7   8   9   10

—You can will yourself to get over the pain.

0   1   2   3   4   5   6   7   8   9   10

—Talking about your pain only makes it worse.

0   1   2   3   4   5   6   7   8   9   10

—You have to grieve alone.

0   1   2   3   4   5   6   7   8   9   10

—Just replace the loss.

0   1   2   3   4   5   6   7   8   9   10

—Anger is sin.

0   1   2   3   4   5   6   7   8   9   10

—If you let yourself feel, you'll be overwhelmed
(or you're a wimp).

0   1   2   3   4   5   6   7   8   9   10

—Don't get close to anyone again. It hurts too much to
lose them.

0   1   2   3   4   5   6   7   8   9   10

—Joy comes in the morning.

0   1   2   3   4   5   6   7   8   9   10

—Memories will always be painful.

0   1   2   3   4   5   6   7   8   9   10

❏ Which one(s) have given you the most confusion and pain? Explain:

❏ Which one(s) still seem like truth to you?

❏ How would it affect you to realize they are myths and reject them?

❏ If you reject these myths, what would you then believe about grief?

Grief is. . .

Stupid Things People Say

I'd had it. I told a friend, "If I hear one more person quote Romans 8:28 to me, I'm going to choke him to death in the name of Jesus!" It's so easy—and so insensitive—for somebody to quote (or misquote) Scripture when he's getting into his car with his family going out to eat after church while I go back to an empty house alone. What they mean is, "Everything is going to work out all right." Oh, yeah? Is it now? Is Cindy going to come out of that grave this afternoon and put our little baby in my arms to hold and feed? That's what "all right" would mean to me. No, it's not going to be "all right." It's tragic. But somehow, God will use the tragedy to deepen me, strengthen me, and share His heart with me. That's what Romans 8:28 is about. Ultimately, God—not fate—prevails.

People say the stupidest things when we have lost someone. I think most of those people mean well, but man alive! They hurt us so deeply by being so insensitive. Of course, each of the myths is a "stupid statement," so we can begin with that list. Here are a few others I've heard:

● "Snap out of it! You've had enough time to feel sorry for yourself."
● "Yeah, I remember when my dog died. I felt the same way you do now."
● "Just be thankful for all you still have."
● "She led a full life."
● "You ought to be happy for him! He's in a better place now!"
● "God will give you somebody even better."
● "My cousin went through the same thing you're going through."
● "A stronger person should be able to handle this."
● "I felt the same way when I went through my divorce. In fact, my pain is worse because I still love my ex-spouse and I still have to see her. At least you know you're wife is dead and buried."
● "You must not be reading your Bible enough."
● "Just pray about it."
● "I bet that really hurt, didn't it?"

● "Maybe that person died so that you would become a Christian. Will you repent now? That would make the death worth it."
● "You just need to get a hold of yourself and cut this crying out."
● "I know exactly how you feel."

❑ What are some stupid things people have said to you?

❑ How did you feel when people said these things to you?

❑ Does it make a difference who said these things to you (close friend or casual acquaintance)?

These comments really hurt me. One of my responses to hearing these insensitive comments was to say to the Lord, "God, I sure hope I've never said anything like this! If I have, please forgive me! And please don't let me ever utter any words like this for the rest of my life!"

❑ What do you plan to say in the future to people who grieve?

Making Plans

Your loved one may have died only recently, or perhaps the death occurred years ago, and you are now entering more fully into the process of grief. Whatever the case, the shock, confusion, hurt, anger, and sadness of our loss often makes it difficult to think clearly. Even though it is difficult, we have responsibilities that require us to think and plan effectively. Take some time to pray, reflect, and plan for the future. I encourage you to talk about your plans to a counselor, pastor, friend, or whoever is helping you through this difficult time.

You will probably want to use additional paper, but this can be a template for you:

Things to consider:
Physical well-being
> Sleep
> Eating habits
> Exercise
> Regulating medications

Emotional well-being
> Time with understanding, supportive people
> Time to cry
> Things I enjoy

Spiritual well-being
> Being honest with God
> Allowing God to be with you in your grief
> Being around supportive believers
> Reentry back into church involvement

Family responsibilities
> Letting others grieve
> Talking to children in the family
> Calls and letters
> Arranging child care

Work, legal, and financial concerns
> Finding the right attorney
> Locating all the assets
> Settling debts
> Insurance claims
> The will

Communicating with family members about the will

Notifying agencies or companies of the death

Getting back to work

Budgeting enough to live on

Setting priorities:

That list looks overwhelming, doesn't it? Many things need to be done, but they don't have to be done today. Set priorities and a schedule you can follow to pace yourself and still get done what needs to be accomplished. List the priorities for these time frames:

❑ Things I need to do this week:

❑ Things I need to do this month:

❑ Things I need to do in the next six months:

❑ Things I need to do in the next year:

Reflection

❑ Read these passages of Scripture. Paraphrase them tell what each one means to you.

Psalm 6:8-9

Psalm 46

Proverbs 3:5-6

❑ Write a prayer expressing your heart to the Lord.
Dear Father,

Step 3
Saying Goodbye

All of us cherish the opportunity to say goodbye to those we love. Long illnesses afford us plenty of time to say what we want to say, but some of us simply can't bring ourselves to say what is on our hearts. In sudden deaths like Cindy's, one of our biggest hurts is that we didn't have that last chance to say, "I love you. You mean so much to me."

Writing a letter to your loved one is a wonderful way to express all you wish you had said. It allows you to think, pray, and speak from your heart. Some of what we want to say to the one we love is to recount all the good times, the happy moments, the meaningful memories. It does our heart good to be thankful for all those things. But perhaps we also need to ask for forgiveness for things we said or did—or things we failed to say or do. If you need to ask for forgiveness, it will help if you consider a role reversal as a response. Think of how you would respond if your loved one sat down and confessed wrongs to you. You would say, "Of course I forgive you. I love you so much! I'm glad you brought it up, and now we can put it behind us. Let's focus from here on the good things." Accept the forgiveness that would be offered, and don't forget, your loved one is one of the "cloud of witnesses" in heaven now. You can be assured of forgiveness!

Thomas Carlyle was a Scottish essayist and poet who, late in life, married Lady Jane Welch. Not long after they were wed, they found out she had a chronic, terminal illness, possibly cancer. Carlyle was a famous man in his day. He traveled the world presenting his work to adoring crowds. When he was at home, he was often focused exclusively on his writing, and he sometimes didn't even see Lady Jane for days on end. The months passed, and eventually, Lady Jane died. She was buried in a country cemetery not far from Carlyle's home.

After the funeral, several friends went with Carlyle back to his house to be with him. He appreciated their friendship, but soon he needed to be alone. He excused himself and walked upstairs to Lady Jane's bedroom. Carlyle sat down in a chair next to her bed. After a few moments, he noticed a book on her night stand. He picked it up. It was her diary. He began to read. Carlyle noticed that on particular days, she put a star next to her entry on the days he came and sat with her. By the stars, she noted things like, "He came by today, and it was like heaven to me! I love him so." Carlyle continued reading. On the last day, when she was barely strong enough to write, there was no star in the diary. He read her words: "The day has grown long, and the shadows are up the hall. I've not heard his footsteps, and I know he'll not be coming today. Oh, how I wish I could tell him I love him so!"

Downstairs, Carlyle's friends were startled when he came tearing down the stairs and bolted out the door. One of them said, "The cemetery! Perhaps he's going to the cemetery." They ran to the graveyard where Lady Jane had been buried only hours earlier. A steady rain was falling now. When they arrived, they found Carlyle lying on the fresh dirt of his wife's grave. He was pounding his fist in the earth saying over and over again, "If I had only known! If I had only known!"

After country singer Reba McIntyre's band was killed in a tragic crash, she wrote a song about a woman's sadness because she turned her head and her beloved husband slipped away. She wishes she had treasured that last walk together, that last talk, that last embrace. The name of that song is "If I Had Only Known."

If I had only known
It was our last walk in the rain
I'd keep you out for hours in the storm
I would hold your hand
Like a lifeline to my heart
Underneath the thunder and the roar
If I had only known
It was the last walk in the rain

If I had only known
I'd never hear your voice again
I'd memorize each thing you ever said
And all those lonely nights
I could think of them once more
And keep your words alive inside my head
If I had only known
I'd never hear you voice again

You were the treasure in my hand
You were the one who always
*   stood beside me*
So unaware, I foolishly believed
*   That you would always be there*
But then there came a day and I
*   Turned my head and you slipped away*

If I had only known
It was my last night by your side
I'd pray a miracle would stop the dawn
And when you smiled at me,
I would look into your eyes
and make sure you know my love for you
*   goes on and on*
If I had only known
If I had only known
The love I would have shown
If I had only known

("If I Had Only Known," Reba McIntyre, from
For My Broken Heart, **used by permission**)

Many of us feel the same pangs. We lament, "If I had only known, this is what I would have said. This is what I would have done for you. Here is how I would have treated you differently." Maybe you had an argument with your spouse or child or parent or friend just before that person died. It's painful to know that the last words spoken were in anger. This is a chance to say something different. So many times, we leave things unsaid. We need to say them now.

❑ Take plenty of time to write a letter to the one you love. The next several pages have the beginnings of statements to help you communicate. Please feel free to change these in any way you choose, and use additional paper if you need it.

I miss you when. . .

My favorite times with you were. . .

I love you because. . .

I'm sorry about. . .

Please forgive me for. . .

I feel. . .

I want you to know. . .

I'm making this commitment to you:

Sharing with others

It is often very helpful to read your letter to your supportive friend or group. They will affirm your feelings and help you process your thoughts and emotions.

Your group or counselor may also invite you to speak to an "empty chair." In this exercise, you imagine your loved one is seated in the chair, and you can say whatever you want to say. The group leader serves as a facilitator to encourage and direct you. This can be a powerfully positive experience—for you and for the whole group.

One of the greatest lessons for me in my grieving over Cindy's death is to realize that every encounter with every person could be the last, so I need to make sure my attitude and words reflect how much I care for each one of them. I used to be a driven, success-oriented person, but I have become a man who savors every moment with his family. It makes a difference. . . a big difference.

❑ Think about the letter you wrote, and the experience of sharing it with your group or friend. How has God used this to help you take the next step in grieving?

❑ Write a prayer to God about this experience.
  Heavenly Father,

Step 4

The Grief Process

We live in an instant society: drive-thru banking, instant credit, on-the-spot news coverage, microwave dinners, and on and on. This is not a culture that knows much about patience and process. Did you ever notice how many of Jesus' parables are about farming? (Now, I know that one reason is that he didn't have a new Pentium II processor in his computer!) The patience and attention required to farm is very similar to many other processes in our lives, including grief. Farming requires plowing, hoeing, planting, weeding, watering, more weeding, waiting, praying for rain, and finally, harvesting. You can't rush the process. It has it's own rhythm, it's own timing.

Many authorities identify stages in the process of grieving. One of the best (and one of the most often used) is a diagram that shows how we move from the initial shock through anger, guilt, depression, and many other points in the process. The last few points, however, show that grief ultimately yields a fruitful harvest of strength and hope.

Loss-Hurt

Loss Adjustment

Shock

Numbness

Denial

Emotional Outbursts

Anger

Fear

Searchings

Disorganization

Panic

Loneliness

Guilt

Helping Others

Affirmation

Hope

New Patterns

New Strengths

New Relationships

"Re-entry" Troubles

Depression

Isolation

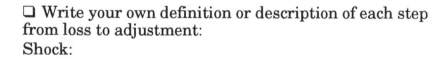 Write your own definition or description of each step from loss to adjustment:

Shock:

Numbness:

Denial:

Emotional outbursts:

Anger:

Fear:

Searchings:

Disorganization:

Panic:

Guilt:

Loneliness:

Isolation:

Depression:

"Re-entry" troubles:

New relationships:

New strengths:

New patterns:

Hope:

Affirmation:

Helping others:

Few of us take a straight line from beginning to end. We move forward a few steps, back one, forward three or four, get stuck for a while, then get going again. We may experience the feelings listed on the diagram at almost anytime. In fact, anger may show up at virtually any point in the process of healing. The behaviors, however, tend to come in the order they are listed.

❑ Circle those you have already experienced.

❑ Put a star next to where you are right now in the process.

❑ Complete this sentence: From what I see on the diagram, in the future I can expect:

Places where we get stuck

It is common to get stuck along the way. We all make progress then fall back, but we don't want to stay stuck for too long. Here are some places many of us get stuck:
● Denial

In his book, *Life on God's Anvil*, Max Lucado records the sad story of a woman, Billie Sicard, who had a child shortly after her husband deserted her. Tragically, her beloved boy, George, died of a brain tumor when he was only twelve. Billie was utterly devastated. She displayed the child's body for a day at a wake in her home, but when the funeral director came to get it, Billie refused to let it go. She mourned for several more days secluded in her home before she let him have George's body. After the funeral, she couldn't bring herself to go into his room to put away his clothes and toys. The days went by, then weeks, then months and years, but Billie Sicard never moved past that tragic day when her son died. A quarter of a century later, George's Cub Scout uniform was still hanging in the front closet. His toys were still scattered around his room. His Mickey Mouse slippers were still on the floor in his bedroom. Only someone in shock would live that way, and this dear woman lived in shock the rest of her life. Her body lived twenty-five more years, but her spirit died that day her son passed away.

Denial doesn't mean we aren't aware the person is dead. It means we can't or won't admit the depth of the meaning of that loss in our lives. We can retreat into a shell.

● Anger

I know a young man who was so distraught at the death of his wife he got stuck in rage for years and years. Hatred and venom poured out of this man on anybody who bumped into him and awakened those awful memories. His anger destroyed virtually every relationship, and eventually, his health.

● Bargaining

Bargaining is swapping one thing for another; I'll do this for you so you'll do that for me. We usually think of bargaining in terms of dysfunctional families in which one person tries to win the love of another by doing everything possible to please that person, but we can also bargain with a deceased person, too. I've talked to men and women who are consumed with the drive to live up to the standards set by their parents. Even after that parent is dead, we keep playing the tapes of that parent's voice in our minds: "You'll never measure up." "Don't let me down." "The whole family is counting on you."

On a plane one day, I talked to a wealthy, powerful businessman who shook his head and told me, "Why do I drive myself so hard? Why do I kill myself to do one more deal and make one more dollar?"

I asked him, "Did your father ever tell you how much he loved you and how proud he was that you were his son?"

The man burst into tears. He whispered, "I could never please him. I've been living my life trying to earn his love."

● Guilt

Some people can never get over the wrongs they did

to the one they love. Some of these are genuine sins of betrayal, adultery, stealing, or other serious wrongs, but other people have extremely sensitive consciences and feel ashamed for not giving one more hug, or failing to call the doctor quite soon enough, or in some other way not preventing the death. Survivor's guilt can be a major problem. I know of a man who felt he needed to marry the wife of a friend who was killed when the car he was driving was in a wreck. Guilt is a powerful motivator . . . but not a healthy one.

● Depression

It can start with feeling disillusioned. We are confused, and we just don't understand all that has happened. That disillusionment can turn to despair, and then to genuine depression, an emotional sink-hole that you think you will be in for the rest of your life.

It is good and right to feel sad. We Christians call self-pity sin, but a friend of mine says that when a person experiences a great loss, self-pity is a natural part of grieving what he has lost. The problem is not the sadness or even the self-pity. The real problem is when these emotions don't subside and aren't replaced with hope and healing.

There are many types of depression. Some are brought on by physiological problems such as tumors or chemical imbalances, but the most common is caused by "anger turned inward." In these cases, people try to suppress the hurt, fear, and anger, but these "stuffed" feelings ultimately control their lives. Depressed people lack energy and creativity. They feel hopeless, helpless, and worthless. Quite often, these people require professional care to get out of the quagmire of depression.

Some of us feel that we should be strong enough in our faith not to struggle with depression, and some of us are so ashamed of being hopeless that we don't get the help we need. If you struggle with depression, please go see your doctor or counselor. They can help you take some positive, specific steps out of this deep hole.

One of the ways depression showed up in my experience was in my inability to sleep. When it came time to go to bed, I could feel the fear rise in my heart. I dreaded laying my head down and closing my eyes because that's when all the thoughts about the hospital experience and the guilt came flooding back into my mind. I often watched television until 3 or 4 in the morning—every morning. By that time, I would fall asleep from exhaustion, but that's not good, restful sleep. Finally, after months of living this way, it all caught up with me. I thought I was having a heart attack. It was an anxiety attack brought on by the combination of my fears and sleep deprivation.

I didn't want to take any medications the doctor prescribed because I am a minister of the gospel, and "I can do all things through Christ who strengthens me." But by the same logic, I shouldn't wear glasses. I tried to handle my pain in the way I thought other people expected me to handle it. I tried to be strong for the church's sake. I only missed one Sunday, and the next week, I came back and preached, "Minoring on the Questions, Majoring on the Answers: Lose yourself in the things you know, and quit asking yourself the things you can't know." That sounds really good, but I wasn't allowing myself the room to be real, to be honest, and to take enough time to feel the pain. I was bottling it up inside of me, and it finally came out in anxiety attacks.

One way to look at each of these "blockages" is to see them as doors to open and walk through. Yes, they are closed at first, but we can open these doors and take the next step in our journey. I believe that all of us come to a stop at these doors. It takes courage, insight, and support to open that door and keep going.

❑ Have you experienced any of these blockages? Explain:

❑ What does a person need to get out of each of these "stuck places"?

Denial—

Bargaining—

Anger—

Guilt—

Depression—

❑ What is the next step for you in the grief process?

❑ What do you need to help you take that step?

❑ What is your part and what is God's part in that step?

❑ Has this study of the process of grief given you more patience and hope? Explain:

❑ What aspects of God's character (love, sovereignty, kindness, wisdom, etc.) have been encouraging to you in the past few days or weeks? Explain:

❑ Express your need to God.
   Lord God, I need You to. . .

Step 5

Finding a Partner

Cindy was dead, and I was in shock. From the waiting room, I called Jerry Vines, my good friend and mentor, because I knew I could say absolutely anything to him. He answered the phone, and I told him about Cindy. He was heartbroken, too. Then, through my tears I said, "Dr. Vines, tell me all this stuff we teach people is really true. I'm having lots of doubts. Every day people go to get rid of babies, and we had prayed and prayed for one. I never thought the answer to our prayer would take my Cindy." Jerry Vines didn't give me a theological discourse on the attributes of God at that moment. He just let me know that he hurt with me, and yes, all the things we teach people is really true.

I hope you already have someone who serves as your partner, friend, and companion in your journey of grieving. If you haven't, I want to encourage you to do whatever you need to do to find that person or group. I've said it before in these pages, and I'll say it again, YOU CANNOT GRIEVE ALONE.

What kind of person do you need? Here are some characteristics to look for:

● A good listener

You need someone who will encourage you to verbalize your feelings and perspectives. There is something wonderful and healing about speaking out loud what is in our hearts. Many times, speaking clarifies what we've been thinking and feeling, and it provides an opportunity for our friend to give us feedback and encouragement. James wrote, "My dear brothers, take note of this: Everyone should be quick to listen, slow to speak, and slow to become angry" (James 1:19).

● Confidentiality

When we grieve, we have thoughts and feelings that aren't pretty and pleasant. We need someone who is safe enough to tell how we honestly feel, and the confidence that person won't go to the next prayer meeting and tell everybody our deepest feelings disguised as a prayer request! Most support groups have a guideline: "Whatever is said in here stays in here." That's a good guideline for any partner, friend or group.

● No simple answers—If someone tells you they can help you get over your pain in some quick, easy way, look for the door! People who have simple answers usually haven't wrestled with deep questions... like death, grief, and emotional healing. Look for people who communicate care first, and answers second (or third!).

● Speaks the truth in love

We need someone who is willing to push us a bit every now and then so we don't get bogged down or stuck. Let me put it this way: We will almost surely get stuck and stay stuck in the grieving process unless someone loves us enough to speak truth to us and lead us by the hand through the door and to the next stage.

Will we always appreciate their honesty? No, we sure won't. We may be quite resistant to taking the next step. Grief can be like a worn leather coat. It's easy to put on and comfortable to keep on. It becomes a protective shield that gives you permission to be angry, depressed, and pitiful. Some people will come around you, pity you and tell you what you want to hear. They'll let you stay stuck, but a true friend will tell you the truth in love, whether you want to hear it or not.

Victor Frankel is the author of *Man's Search for Meaning*. All his family except one sister died in Nazi concentration camps. He watched men and women live day after day in those horribly oppressive conditions, and he drew some conclusions about the ones who lived and the ones who didn't. He said, "I came to the realization that the last human freedom we have is our ability to choose our attitude in any given set of circumstances." Some, he observed, don't want to survive. And for some, the camp provided an excuse for them to complain and blame, and to be cynical and hateful. Each of us can choose to take steps forward instead of taking the easy way of staying stuck in our anger and self-pity.

Men have a natural tendency to be tough. They believe if they don't think about the pain, it'll go away. But that simply won't happen. The repressed hurt and anger will show up in irritability, dumb decisions, withdrawal from meaningful relationships, or being driven to prove themselves.

● Available

Some people may be highly qualified to be your partner in grief, but they don't have enough time to help you. Quite often, those who can comfort are sought by lots of people who hurt. Being a partner is a genuine commitment that requires time and energy. If a person or two is unable to make that commitment, don't despair. The Lord will provide someone. Keep looking until He does.

Don't look for "the perfect grief partner." That person doesn't exist. Psychologist Virginia Satir wrote years ago about our need for nurturing parents. She said we don't need perfect parents, just "good enough parents." You and I don't need perfect friends to help us; we need "good enough friends."

Where can you find someone like this? One lady told me she thought she had found a friend to help her, but after a couple of weeks, this person told her she was "too needy" for her. Don't be surprised if people can't handle your pain. They may have never gone through a tragedy like yours, so all they have to offer are simple answers. If you don't respond to these answers and "get fixed," they quickly run out of tricks. You may have to look for a while to find the right person or the right group. Here are some places to look:

● Someone you know who has walked the path

Do you know someone who has experienced loss and

successfully gone through the grief process? That person may be your first and best choice to walk by your side. This may be someone you have known only from a distance, but you've heard about this person's journey of grief. The exact situations don't have to be similar. That person my have lost a child and you lost a spouse. That doesn't matter. The important thing is to find someone who empathizes with your pain and is willing to walk the path with you.

● Your pastor

In the earliest days of your loss, lean on your pastor for comfort, insight, and strength. Ask your pastor if he (or she) knows someone who can be an ongoing grief partner for you, or if there is a grief support group in the church or the community.

● Grief support group

Many hospitals offer grief support groups targeted for specific types of losses (such as the death of a child or the death of a spouse). Also, many churches offer groups like this. I strongly encourage you to find a group to join. You will gain so much by listening to others share their trials and joys. Looking into the eyes of those who understand and care means so much, and the honest feedback they give you will help you take the next step at each moment of the journey.

● A Christian counselor

God led me to a godly Christian counselor who helped me tremendously. Dr. Ron Braund listened patiently and helped me sort out the jumble of intense emotions I felt. He skillfully asked me questions to clarify my thinking and draw out my feelings, and at certain points, he pushed me a little bit to help me take a step I needed to take.

A Christian counselor shares your values and understands how the life of the Spirit influences your grieving process. Ask your pastor or support group leader for names of counselors in your area.

● A combination of people

Most people who successfully navigate the grief process have many people who play important roles. I encourage you to have at least one individual (a friend, pastor, or counselor) to meet with you one-on-one, and join a group for the benefit of learning and growing in that powerful, nurturing context.

In all these environments, tell your story of heartache and hope. Use this book and workbook as a template for you and your group.

● Read

Take time to read other people's stories of loss and grief. These will give you additional insights, and you will gain strength from learning how these people overcame the deep hurts they experienced.

Remember that you are the one responsible for your own grieving and growing. No one can do that for you, but you can't do it alone. Supportive people are worth their weight in gold at this time in your life. Don't stop looking until you've found people who will walk with you in this time of need.

❑ Who do you know who has gone through the deep grief of losing a loved one?

❑ Which of these people has grieved that loss and found hope and healing?

❑ Describe why you need someone who. . .
is a good listener:

can keep your thoughts and feelings confidential:

speaks the truth in love:

is available:

❏ What does it mean to be a "good enough friend" in helping you? (What might be some unrealistic expectations someone might have of a grief partner?)

❏ Where are some grief support groups in your area?

❏ How can you get information about other groups?

❑ Who are some competent, Christian counselors in your area? (Who can give you the names of some?)

❑ At what point does a person need to contact a professional counselor to help you?

❑ What are some reasons a grieving person might resist help from a friend, pastor, group, or counselor?

❑ Has grieving become "comfortable, like a worn leather coat" to you? Why or why not?

❏ Read Isaiah 40:27-31. Paraphrase each verse:

Verse 27:

Verse 28:

Verse 29:

Verse 30:

Verse 31:

❑ Is your experience today more like verse 27: "My way is hidden from the Lord; my cause is disregarded by my God," or like verse 31: ". . . they will soar on wings like eagles"? Explain.

❏ Express your heart to the Lord.
  My Father, I feel. . .

I want. . .

I will. . .

Step 6
Necessary Adjustments

Those who lose someone in a long, lingering illness have time to anticipate the adjustments that need to be made when the person dies, and in many cases, some of the decisions can be made ahead of time. However, many of us are so preoccupied with caring for that person, or in denial about the impending death, that we fail to be adequately prepared. In sudden deaths, of course, there is no time to anticipate anything. The blow is overwhelming, and decisions have to be made in the fog of confusion and shock.

A major part of the grief process is determining what we are responsible for and what we aren't—what we need to do on our own and what we need help to accomplish. For instance, we need to take responsibility for our finances, and we are responsible to let others grieve, too. But we probably need an attorney to help probate the will, and we need a friend to be with us when we go through the child's room for the first time.

Here are some Do's and Don'ts in making these adjustments:

Do:

✔ Be honest with yourself, with God, and with at least one other person about your feelings.

✔ Plan. Make a priority list of the things that need to be done and a schedule for getting them accomplished.

✔ Find a support system of a pastor, friend, counselor, or group (or some combination of these).
✔ Be patient. Don't expect to "get over it" quickly. Have realistic expectations of yourself and others as you grieve.
✔ Embrace the reality of the loss so you can genuinely grieve.
✔ Take care of your physical well-being. Eat right, exercise, and get the rest you need.
✔ Read the Psalms to reflect on David's (and other psalmists') feelings and reflections about God and life.
✔ Help others grieve, especially family members. Speak to children on their level, but be honest with them about your pain.
✔ Identify the places when you get stuck so you can open that door and keep going.
✔ Learn to laugh again.
✔ Find some things you enjoy.
✔ Thank those who care for being there for you.

Don't:
✗ Bottle up your emotions.
✗ Withdraw from family and friends.
✗ Condemn yourself for being weak.
✗ Be impatient with yourself for needing time to grieve or for going backwards from time to time.
✗ Deny physical symptoms of stress such as frequent headaches and recurring gastro-intestinal problems.
✗ Fail to plan adequately.
✗ Rush into important decisions.
✗ Avoid important decisions because they are painful.
✗ Yell at people when they say stupid things to you about your loss.
✗ Continue to blame yourself or others for the death.

There are many difficult adjustments you may need to make. One of these might be becoming a single parent. In this case, you will take on the roles of both father and mother. One is stressful enough, but now you have both roles as well as the pain of losing a spouse. Be sure to find help. Maybe a grandparent can help shoulder the burden and provide relief for you and nurture for your children. Perhaps you need to find others in the community to give you some help in this difficult, daunting task of being a single parent. Take care of yourself physically so you have the strength you need to take care of your increased responsibilities.

I've seen disastrous situations involving money after a person's death. On some occasions, a husband has died suddenly and his grieving wife is in a fog emotionally. In addition, she is in a financial fog because he has left her with no knowledge at all about the family finances: savings, stocks, life insurance (perhaps with a burial policy), other investments, and all kinds of debts. Women in these circumstances don't even know where to look to see how much money they have to live on. In these cases, I encourage them to find a good, competent CPA or a lawyer to help track down the finances and explain the situation. He can also make recommendations about the best course of action to pay off debts and establish a livable income.

A wonderful friend of mine was an airline pilot who was the picture of health. One day he was in the cockpit telling a story, and he stopped just before the punch line. The co-pilot said, "Go ahead. What happened next?" Then he looked over, and my friend was dead from a sudden, massive heart attack. This man had his finger in many different businesses and investments, but his wife was not involved in the day-to-day operations. She was devastated by his death, and she was also dazed as she began to find bits and pieces of information about his investments and business dealings. I got her together with a good lawyer and a CPA who put all the pieces of the puzzle together for her. Their help was invaluable in giving her the information and advice she needed to make good decisions.

Another adjustment for a surviving spouse is to learn to relate to friends without the deceased spouse. Their identity has been as a couple, but now, how will the couples relate to the one left behind? I've seen other couples withdraw from the surviving spouse and hurt that person deeply, but I've also seen many instances of couples communicating, "We're so sorry your spouse died. We'll miss him (or her) so much too. We want to reaffirm our friendship with you. We know things won't quite be the same, but we want to be your friends. Will you come over for dinner tomorrow night?" That kind of sentiment—and that kind of action to back up the sentiment—does a world of good to provide strength and stability to the grieving spouse. The problem, however, may not be the friends' reluctance to relate to the surviving spouse. The survivor may not want to relate to other couples because it reminds that person of the deep loss and loneliness.

Birthdays, anniversaries, and other special dates can be incredibly difficult. We remember the wonderful times together, and those memories awaken our deep hurts again. Sometimes we anticipate those dates with a sense of forboding. These dates represent very important times in your life. Don't run from them. Feel the sadness, but focus on the good times and thank God for them. That won't make the sadness go away, but it will at least soften the pain.

The first holidays after a death are usually the worst. The intense feelings of loss are raw and bleeding. Be sure to be with others during that time who will support and affirm you. This, too, is an important part of the grief process. For some people, these first holidays are the first time they let themselves truly embrace the depth of their loss. This point is terribly painful, but it is a crucial step forward.

The toughest days for many of us are the days the person died and the day the person was buried. We relive those days as if they happened only yesterday—or maybe today. Again, don't run from these feelings. Let them connect you to that person you love without letting that connection overwhelm you. That's difficult at first, but as time goes on, you can embrace those memories with both joy and sadness, and they will be stepping stones in your healing.

Many support groups use a simple, clear method of making adjustments. The method includes five steps:
1. Gain awareness
2. Accept responsibility for decisions
3. Define appropriate recovery communications, such as forgiving, telling your story, saying "thank you," or making amends
4. Take action
5. Move beyond the experience by sharing it with others.

These groups use an acronym "AARAM" to help them remember what they need to do:

Awareness

Accept

Recovery

Action

Move

❑ Which of the "Do's" are you accomplishing now?

❑ Which of the "Do's" stand out to you as things you need to concentrate on?

❑ How will concentrating on these help you as you make necessary adjustments?

❑ Which of the "Don'ts" are you avoiding already?

❑ Which ones do you need to concentrate on avoiding?

❑ How will that help you?

❑ What are some adjustments you need to make at this point regarding:
Finances:

Legal matters:

Children and child care:

Your physical health:

Sleep and exercise:

Major decisions (like selling the house and moving or getting a job):

Relationships with friends:

Birthdays, anniversaries, holidays, and other special dates:

❏ Think through the AARAM method for each one:

❑ For the next week, keep a journal to record your thoughts, feelings, goals, and prayers. (You may be keeping a journal already.) You may choose to journal in the morning, or you may want to reflect before you go to bed. Consider using these "statement starters" to focus your thoughts:

Day 1
The high point of my day was. . .

The low point was. . .

Right now I feel. . .

My goals for the upcoming day are. . .

To accomplish these, I need. . .

The "Do's" I need to focus on are. . .

The "Don'ts" I need to focus on are. . .

A passage of Scripture that has been meaningful to me today is: Explain.

Heavenly Father, I feel. . .

I want. . .

I will. . .

Day 2
The high point of my day was. . .

The low point was. . .

Right now I feel. . .

My goals for the upcoming day are. . .

To accomplish these, I need. . .

The "Do's" I need to focus on are. . .

The "Don'ts" I need to focus on are. . .

A passage of Scripture that has been meaningful to me today is: Explain.

Heavenly Father, I feel. . .

I want. . .

I will. . .

Day 3
The high point of my day was. . .

The low point was. . .

Right now I feel. . .

My goals for the upcoming day are. . .

To accomplish these, I need. . .

The "Do's" I need to focus on are. . .

The "Don'ts" I need to focus on are. . .

A passage of Scripture that has been meaningful to me today is: Explain.

Heavenly Father, I feel. . .

I want. . .

I will. . .

Day 4

The high point of my day was. . .

The low point was. . .

Right now I feel. . .

My goals for the upcoming day are. . .

To accomplish these, I need. . .

The "Do's" I need to focus on are. . .

The "Don'ts" I need to focus on are. . .

A passage of Scripture that has been meaningful to me today is: Explain.

Heavenly Father, I feel. . .

I want. . .

I will. . .

Day 5
The high point of my day was. . .

The low point was. . .

Right now I feel. . .

My goals for the upcoming day are. . .

To accomplish these, I need. . .

The "Do's" I need to focus on are. . .

The "Don'ts" I need to focus on are. . .

A passage of Scripture that has been meaningful to me today is: Explain.

Heavenly Father, I feel. . .

I want. . .

I will. . .

Day 6
The high point of my day was. . .

The low point was. . .

Right now I feel. . .

My goals for the upcoming day are. . .

To accomplish these, I need. . .

The "Do's" I need to focus on are. . .

The "Don'ts" I need to focus on are. . .

A passage of Scripture that has been meaningful to me today is: Explain.

Heavenly Father, I feel. . .

I want. . .

I will. . .

Day 7
The high point of my day was. . .

The low point was. . .

Right now I feel. . .

My goals for the upcoming day are. . .

To accomplish these, I need. . .

The "Do's" I need to focus on are. . .

The "Don'ts" I need to focus on are. . .

A passage of Scripture that has been meaningful to me today is: Explain.

Heavenly Father, I feel. . .

I want. . .

I will. . .

❑ How have you seen God at work in your life in the past seven days?

❑ What have you learned in the past seven days about grief, about yourself, and about God?

Step 7
Overcoming Guilt

Few of us (if any) experience the death of someone we love without feeling some pangs of guilt. Do you remember the story of Thomas Carlyle finding his wife's diary entry of her disappointment that he had not come to visit her, along with her undying love for him. Carlyle ran to his wife's freshly dug grave and beat his fists into the dirt, saying, "If only I had known! If only I had known!"

Many of us have these "if only's":
- If only we'd had more time.
- If I'd only said "I love you" before he died.
- If only I hadn't lied.
- If only I hadn't stopped for that cup of coffee.
- If only I had not run that red light.
- If only I'd taken him to the doctor earlier.
- If only I hadn't been such a jerk to her.
- If only I had it to do all over again.
- If only I'd asked for forgiveness.

Some of our "if only's" are regrets about fate. When I was a boy, my brother Sonny and my cousin Gene were going to pick up their dates in Robbinsville, North Carolina. As they were driving off, I ran and stopped them and asked if I could go along. Sonny said, "No, you can't go on a date with us! You're too young." They drove off, and on the drive to Robbinsville, they had a wreck. When I heard about it, I thought, "If I hadn't asked if I could go along, they wouldn't have had that wreck. The timing would have been off. It's all my fault."

In the same way, if we had asked for a C-section for Cindy, she wouldn't have had the amniotic embolism that killed her. If I hadn't wanted a child, she wouldn't have gotten pregnant and she wouldn't have died. Those were my "if only's" in Cindy's death, and the guilt almost drove me crazy. We can't dwell on those things that are good honest decisions but turn out to be a factor in a tragedy.

Other "if only's" are about wrongs we've done that person. We feel guilty about causing the other person harm by our thoughtlessness, our selfishness, and our blatant sins. These haunt us because they didn't have to happen. We are genuinely at fault.

"If only's" can be dangerous. They can lock us into the past and keep us stuck in self-condemnation. They can be an agent for good only if we realize they, too, are something we need to grieve. If we grieve them, they can become a powerful, positive force in future relationships and actions. For instance, I told Cindy I loved her just before I walked out of the room before she went into cardiac arrest, but I felt guilty for being so driven and preoccupied during that time of my life. I had a lot of "if only" guilt feelings for a while, then I allowed God to use them to make me aware of being so driven. I repented. Today, I treasure every single moment with my family. I'm not nearly so driven as before. I think I'm a better husband and father today because I allowed God to use that "if only" guilt to point me in a new direction.

There can be forgiveness and resolution for those sins we committed that hurt the other person, too. We can confess our sin to God and to our partner and support group, and experience forgiveness. We can write a letter or speak to "the empty chair" to express our contrition and repentance. If you do this, think of how you would respond if the tables were turned and your loved one came to you with a repentant heart. . . and accept that forgiveness.

There's one other scenario for "if only's." Some of us were wronged deeply by the person who died, and we lament, "If only my Dad had shown love to me," or "If only my husband had been faithful." In these situations, the person's death effectively ends any chance of him changing and giving us the love, time, honesty, and care we desperately wanted from him. We now need to grieve two wounds: the loss of hope that he will change and love us, and his death, too.

I believe Satan loves to heap guilt on you and me in the "if only's." The Holy Spirit convicts us of sin and focuses on the things that can be changed, but the Devil focuses his long, boney fingers on those things that can't be changed and says, "You're awful! It's all your fault! You're no good at all!" He'll beat you up emotionally by bringing all the "if only's" up in your mind over and over again. . . until you join him in self-flagellation. The "if only's" keep us stuck in the past where things can't be changed. We then miss out on the love of the present and the hope for the future. People who dwell in the past are sullen, bitter people, and this bitterness shapes their relationships because others don't want to be around someone so negative and sour.

Survivors wonder, "Why me? Why did that person die and I was spared? It doesn't make sense. It's not fair!" I wondered why God took Cindy instead of me when she loved him more than I did. She was more vivacious and more charming than I could ever be. Why? Why? Why? A parent who watches a child die wonders, "Why my precious child and not me? I've lived. I've had my chance, but my precious child was taken without the chance to truly live."

And survivors struggle with guilt when they are happy. They think, "I don't deserve to be happy when my wife (or husband or child or. . .) is dead. It's not fair to them." Survivors feel they don't deserve to have a meaningful life, or to have anything good—because anything good in our lives makes it seem that other person's life is meaningless or that we didn't care. If survivors have a new relationship, it somehow seems that their relationship with the deceased person wasn't so important. When Robin and I began to date, I had to wrestle with these feelings. And there were people who wanted to make sure I wrestled with them! I could hear them mutter, "Well, he's sure happy now. . . and so soon, too." Some of Cindy's friends felt that I betrayed them and I betrayed Cindy's memory by dating Robin and finding new happiness. I want to tell you, the person who would have been happiest about Robin is Cindy (and I suspect she saw it all looking over the parapets of heaven). Survivors are afraid of betraying the memory of that person who died, and they get bogged down in guilt and unhappiness to make sure they don't betray that person.

Why do ten people survive a plane crash when 200 die? I don't know. Why does one person in a car wreck live when three others die? I don't know. But those who live need to realize that God has a purpose in allowing them to live. That purpose is that they honor Him in everything they think, say, and do. It may be much more specific than that, but true discipleship is a worthy purpose for all of us believers.

If we don't identify the guilt, it can consume us. The downward spiral of disillusionment and despair is compounded with self-hatred for somehow contributing to the death, and depression soon follows. The depths of depression are actually safer and more attractive for some of us than "good grief" because depression provides us with the excuse for self-pity, rage, and apathy. It takes tremendous courage to face our guilt—real or imagined—and make choices to move forward.

❑ What "if only" thoughts have you had. . .
about fate?

about wrongs you did to the person?

about wrongs that person did to you?

❑ Has your guilt "haunted you"? Explain:

❑ Define and describe "survivor's guilt":

❑ Have you felt guilty for being happy or having something meaningful or beautiful in your life? Explain:

❑ Forgiving yourself—Read Colossians 2:13-15.
How many of your sins has Christ forgiven (verse 13)?

What price did He pay (verse 14)?

What proof did he offer (verse 15)?

❑ Read Luke 15:11-32.
What wrongs did the prodigal son commit?

What does it mean "he came to his senses"?

Describe the scene when his father saw him down the road:

How did the father forgive and welcome him back?

❑ If God forgives so warmly and so fully, what prevents you from accepting that forgiveness right now?

Imagine yourself as the prodigal son returning to a loving, forgiving father. Express your acceptance of his love:

❑ Forgiving others—Read Matthew 21-35.
How large was the servant's debt to the king? Could he repay it?

How great is your debt to God? Can you ever repay it?

What did this servant ask for? What did the king grant him?

Why was the king's servant so harsh with his fellow servant over his small debt?

❏ What are some of the damaging effects of not forgiving others (on you, on your relationships, emotional health, physical well-being, etc.)?

❏ Read Ephesians 4:32.
To what extent are we to forgive others?

❑ As you experience the forgiveness of Christ, you will be willing and able to forgive others for the wrongs they have done to you. Forgiveness is not based on a feeling. It is a choice. What will help you experience Christ's forgiveness more?

❑ Express your forgiveness of those who have wronged you. Be specific; list each person and the wrongs they have done to hurt you.

❑ Express your heart to the Lord.
Father, thank you for forgiving me for. . .

I choose to forgive those who have hurt me when they. . .

❑ Talk to your partner, pastor, counselor, or group about your experience in this exercise to gain more insight and encouragement.

Step 8
New Hope

As we continue to take steps, day after day, in our grieving process, we will grow stronger. We will be able to find new meaning in life, new hope, new joys. In this process, we will also be quicker to identify unhealthy coping mechanisms which bog us down. Here are a few of those unhealthy ways we have tried to cope:

● Retreating into busyness

To avoid facing the pain, many of us do almost anything to occupy our time and our minds. We spend long hours at the office, we dive into a multitude of projects around the house, we lose ourselves in television, we read incessantly. . . anything to avoid thinking and feeling.

● Becoming and expert

Especially in prolonged illnesses, some people read and study to become an expert on the disease. Of course, there's nothing wrong with being informed, but many of these people think they can somehow do enough to prevent their loved one's death. Those who do so much to help the person live may be the most devastated when their loved one dies.

● Shallow, incomplete grief

"I'm just fine." "No problem." "Doing a lot better now." These and other statements may be an honest appraisal, but often, they are a cover for incomplete grief. We want to believe our pain is over, and we tell ourselves and others that it doesn't hurt anymore. . . even though it is killing us.

● Inappropriate humor

I'm all for a good laugh, but some of us use humor to cover our pain. To avoid hurting—and to avoid our hurt being revealed to others—we tell jokes when people want to console us, and we laugh when we ought to cry.

● Explosions of anger, blaming, complaining

It's a lot easier to get mad than it is to grieve. Just days after Cindy died, I had several lawyers call me offering to help me sue the hospital. They wanted me to "make those suckers pay." I couldn't do that. I wasn't tempted at all because I know those men and women did all they could possibly do to save Cindy's life. They weren't at fault any more than I was at fault. Blaming and complaining would only have gotten my focus off my own, personal loss and put it on getting revenge. Anger is powerful. It gives us energy and identity. It allows us to say, "I'm the one who was wronged. I'm the one who deserves better. I'm the one you should take care of." But that's not grief.

Watch for triggers in your life, such as a collapse of health, self-destructive thoughts, prolonged confusion, or helplessness. If these are acute or if they persist, be sure to tell your group or partner so you can get the help you need.

Christians have questions about where God was when their loved one got sick or died accidentally. They don't understand how God could allow that to happen. But the Father was in the same place He was when His Son died. He was watching and caring. Even Jesus felt abandoned in that hour of darkness. He cried out, "My God, my God! Why have You forsaken me?" There is such loneliness and despair in that plea. He felt abandoned by the One He knew loved Him. . . just as we can feel abandoned by the God we know loves us.

There's nothing wrong with doubting God. The Psalms are full of honest expressions of doubt, hurt, despair, and disillusionment. If the people you talk to are not comfortable with your doubts and questions, then maybe you need to find someone else who understands. At the end of his ministry, John the Baptist was in prison awaiting execution. He had doubts about Jesus, so he sent his disciples to Jesus to find out if he was truly the Messiah. He told them to ask if He is the one or if they should look for someone else. These men saw Jesus heal the sick, raise the dead, and make the blind see. They returned to tell their doubting leader, and John was satisfied that Jesus was for real. That encourages me! If John the Baptist, whom Jesus said was "greatest in the kingdom of heaven" doubted Jesus, then it's okay for me to doubt, too. And somehow, some way, Jesus will get word to me, too, that He is for real. For John the Baptist—and for you and me—unexpected circumstances brought unaccustomed emotions. His doubts, coupled with his honesty and his search for truth, led him to a stronger faith in God. I'm really glad God put that passage in the Bible.

Jesus Himself didn't want to face the physical and spiritual pain of crucifixion. He prayed, "Father, if You will, let this cup pass." He wanted to avoid that pain just as a we want to avoid the pain of a child dying from leukemia or a parent dying from chronic heart disease. He expressed His fears and hopes, but the Father said, "No. You have to go through it."

We know that God is just. We may not understand why He does some things, but we can be sure He is kind, gracious, and near. We may not always feel He is near, but we can be confident that He is as close as our breath. God is sovereign and omniscient. He is never surprised. Nothing happens by accident. The only thing that can interrupt His plan for each of us are our own misguided choices, and even then, He can bring us back and give us new meaning. He has a purpose in all things.

Sometimes, being in the center of God's will is the most bewildering thing we can experience. We think God's will is always crystal clear, but if you think that, consider Job. He was totally confused (and his friends didn't help much either!) about God and His purposes, but God broke through and shared His heart to comfort Job. I can imagine Job saying to God, "Next time you want to think of me, find somebody else! The last time you brought my name up, all hell broke loose! The only thing I had left was the one thing I wanted to get rid of— my wife!" But Job gained insight from his difficulties, and his conclusion (in spite of his wife's advice to "curse God and die") was "Though He slay me, yet will I trust Him."

Job asked the question of the ages, "If a man dies, will he live?" And the answer is, "Yes!" The resurrection of Jesus Christ came out of the crucifixion—the best event came from the worst event in human history. The One who knew no sin became sin to pay for sin, so that you and I might be assigned His own righteousness and right standing as sons and daughters of God. Ultimately then, our hope is in God Himself and His gracious promise to resurrect those who trust in Him. That gives meaning, purpose, endurance, and true hope. Jesus spent three days in the dark grave. You and I may spend many months in the darkness of confusion, despair, and desperation, but sooner or later the light of life comes. The answers we need are not about the event of the death. The answers are in the character of God. The great 19th century English preacher, Charles Haddon Spurgeon stated, "God is too good to be unkind. He is too wise to be mistaken. When I cannot trace His hand, I can always trust His heart."

❏ On a scale of 0 (not at all) to 10 (all the time), how much have you used these unhealthy coping mechanisms?

Retreating into busyness
0   1   2   3   4   5   6   7   8   9   10
Becoming and expert
0   1   2   3   4   5   6   7   8   9   10
Shallow, incomplete grief
0   1   2   3   4   5   6   7   8   9   10
Inappropriate humor
0   1   2   3   4   5   6   7   8   9   10
Explosions of anger, blaming, complaining
0   1   2   3   4   5   6   7   8   9   10

❑ What have been some of the effects of using these?

❑ What doubts have you had about God during your grief?

❑ How have you felt about having these doubts?

❑ How did you feel as you read the paragraphs about John the Baptist doubting, Jesus feeling betrayed, and Jesus getting a "No" answer from the Father?

❑ Read Psalm 139.
Paraphrase the meaning of these sections:
Verses 1-6:

Verses 7-12:

Verses 13-16:

Verses 17-18:

Verses 19-22:

Verses 23-24:

❑ Write a letter to God about your reflections from this passage of Scripture and what it means to you in this time in your life.

Step 9

Talking to Family and Friends

Some families talk about everything: hopes, fears, the tomatoes, roaches, the high school football game this weekend, Aunt Jean's rheumatism. . . . You get the idea. But just because they've talked about things up to now doesn't mean they will share their hurts about a death in the family. They have a good track record, but they may need someone in the family to have the courage to take the first step.

Of course, some families don't talk about anything but the weather (if that!). They hide behind newspapers and squat in front of television sets. Their bodies may be in the same room, but their hearts are poles apart. These families will have a difficult time talking about the hurts and fears of the recent death.

You need to talk about your hurts more for them than for yourself. They worry about you, and they need to know that you are in the process of grieving. I've only seen my father cry one time: that was when Cindy died. But Dad was worried about whether I would survive the intense pain that was etched on my face.

Talking to them is a part of loving them, and it's a way to let them love you. Don't shove them out. Certainly, it's easy to focus on our own needs when we've lost someone, but we will all benefit if we open up and let someone care about us.

Some of us think we need to do it perfectly, that we

have to say just the right words to our families. We're afraid we'll burst into tears and blurt out something we'll wish we hadn't said. Don't worry about that. Unless you are enraged at someone in the family, you can blurt out your pain and hurt and let them comfort you. They may blurt and cry just as much or more than you because they care so much.

If someone in your family begins to give advice, tell you how you ought to feel, or fix you in some other way, quietly say, "Thanks, but I'm not ready to hear that right now. Maybe later. I'll let you know. Right now, all I want is to know you care. Thanks for being here for me." Remember, your family members hurt, too. They need comfort, strength, and to hear the truth in love just like you do.

Try to avoid reacting to any stupid things people might blurt out in their grief. For example, someone may say, "My grief is worse than anybody else's." Let that person think and feel that way without correcting her. From her perspective, she's right. She can't imagine anybody hurting worse than she hurts. And don't bother to correct a person's theology. Sometimes I hear a person say, "I know my wife's an angel now. She's looking down on me, taking care of me." Well, people don't become angels when they die, but the grieving person doesn't need a discourse on angelology at that particular moment. Let it go.

Especially in the early stages, it will take great concentration and effort for you to listen to others' pain and not focus exclusively on your own. There is a temptation to compare shark bites of pain like the old salts did in *Jaws*: "See this scar? A great white got me there." "Oh yeah, well this scar on me is bigger, and the shark was bigger, too!" We're not in this to out-hurt each other, competing to see who has slept the least, cried the most, and has gone to the cemetery the most times. Push yourself to listen, to ask second and third questions to draw people out, and to listen even more.

Children need special care during times of grief. I remember telling a little boy that his father had died. I said, "Son, you're Dad has died. He's in heaven now." The boy looked up at me and said, "Then I want to go to heaven, too."

Here are some principles to help children deal with death:

● Tell them the truth. Don't assume they can't handle it. Children are much more resilient than we may think, and they appreciate honesty.

● Share your own grief with them. Be a part of one another's support structure. You will be your child's role model of sharing grief—or suppressing those emotions.

● Allow the child to go through the grief process, including anger, hurt, discouragement, and recovery.

● Listen. Listen. Listen. Ask follow up questions instead of giving simple answers. When it's time to give answers, help the child discover some of them on his own by being a part of family discussions.

● Continue familiar routines to provide stability.

● Reassure the child about the future.

● Communicate positive stories and memories about the deceased person.

● Be aware of any danger signals in the child's moods or behavior, such as lack of sleep, outbursts of anger, psychosomatic illnesses, etc.

● Don't look to the child to be your primary source of comfort. That's too much responsibility for a child.

● Be patient. Let the child cry without correcting her.

● Over time, allow the experience to be a platform of new hope, new insights, and new strength.

Young children (preschoolers) may not grasp the significance of the death. They may think the person has gone on a trip to a place called "heaven." Don't push too hard. They'll understand later. Allow children to go to the funeral so they can see what is going on. Even if they don't understand what has happened, they will see that people are saying goodbye.

Children 6 to 9 years old are beginning to understand the finality of death. They often have very specific questions about what is going on in the grave, for instance, how the dead person can breathe and eat. Patiently explain what has happened—many times if necessary. Some children fantasize about their own deaths. Don't be too alarmed, but reassure the child and provide nurture and comfort.

Children 10 to 12 years old are formulating their conceptions of life and death. Some at this age are very mature in their understanding, but others respond more like younger children. They often want more information about death, so you may want to anticipate this need by explaining the events surrounding death and burial, or provide a book or article for them to read.

Pre-teens and teenagers are growing in their awareness of spiritual matters. You can communicate honestly and deeply with them about eternity, but they may not be able yet to express their feelings very well.

For all ages, be patient and kind in your communication with them. They are grieving in their own ways. Expect them to go through the stages of grief at their own pace and with their own expressions of hurt and hope.

❑ Analyze your family's communication style. Which people normally communicate deeply and well about heart issues? Which ones withdraw? Which ones blame?

❑ And your close friends? Which ones communicate well? . . . withdraw? . . . blame?

❑ List each member of your family and your close friends. Describe how each one has responded to the death of your loved one.

❑ Which of these have you resisted talking to about the death? What are your reasons?

❑ Which of them would benefit from talking with you?

❑ When do you plan to talk to them?

❑ Write out your plan so you will be prepared.
What do you want to communicate?
What are your fears in talking to that person?
How can you prepare yourself for that person's anger, blaming, self-pity, etc.?

❑ List the children who grieve this death, and describe how each one has handled the loss:

❑ Think back on deaths in the family that occurred when you were a child. How old were you? How did your parents help you handle your grief? What did you learn to do (or avoid doing) for children as a result of this experience?

❏ Look at the list of principles on how to communicate with children, then write out a plan of how you want to talk to each one.

❏ When do you plan to talk to them?

❏ Complete this statement: I can help my family and friends grieve by. . .

❏ The Scriptures indicate that our attitudes and actions are an overflow of what is in our hearts.
Read John 7: 37-39 and paraphrase it here:

❑ Read I John 4:9-11, Romans 15:7, and Ephesians 4:32. What do these passages say is our motivation and source to be able to love, accept, and forgive others?

❑ Express your heart to the Father about your desire to help others grieve.
   Heavenly Father, I want. . .

I commit myself to. . .

Thank You for. . .

Step 10

Who Am I Now?

God made us for relationships, and our sense of identity is inextricably linked to those relationships. Our bonds with others powerful and positive, but they are painful when they are broken. Quite often, the sense of who we are is closely connected with the person who has died:

"I'm Jim's wife."

"I'm Kathleen's father."

"I'm Bill's sister."

"I'm Sarah's mother."

"I'm Joyce's friend."

When that person dies, the cord that ties us to that person seems to be severed, and we feel cast adrift, wondering who we are and where we belong. This feeling is often compounded by the fact that the death may have changed how we relate to other people. If a child has died, other parents may not know what to say to us, so they avoid contact with us. If a spouse has died, other couples that were friends may not feel comfortable with us as new singles. And of course, they may feel perfectly comfortable. . . but we may not! In addition, the blow to our identity is further complicated by our fresh and raw feelings of guilt, hurt, shock, confusion, and anger. We feel disconnected at the very time we need people the most.

One woman asked me sadly after her husband died, "Now that Frank's gone, I don't know who I am since I'm not a wife any more."

I responded, "Of course you're Frank's wife."

Her eyes lit up.

"And you'll always be Frank's wife. That doesn't change just because he died."

Somehow, that simple insight gave her a new sense of stability. She hadn't lost her identity. She had experienced a great loss when her husband died, but she was still his wife. That gave her comfort.

Many circumstances in life threaten our sense of identity:

● When the children all have left home, the "empty nest syndrome" makes parents look at each other and wonder, "Who are we now? What do we do every day?"

● When a person retires, his identity is no longer tied up in a job title, performance, or work relationships. That is a major blow to those who have invested their entire sense of who they are in that job.

● Passing through the stages of life can shake us up. Moving away from home, getting married, middle age, and losing vitality in old age threaten our perceptions about ourselves.

● Major transitions in life also can be blows to our emotional stability: changing jobs, getting divorced, moving to another city, having children, and changes in our financial status (either up or down) make us reconsider our identity.

Through all of these, and especially when someone close to us has died, we need to focus on the one true constant of our identity: who we are in Christ. No matter what winds rip our sails and rock our boats, the fact that we are loved, forgiven, accepted children of God doesn't change one iota. Even if everything else around us changes, that doesn't. Psalm 46 expresses this strong view:

> God is our refuge and strength,
> an ever-present help in trouble.

Therefore we will not fear, though the earth
    give way
and the mountains fall into the heart of the
    sea,
though its waters roar and foam
    and the mountains quake with their
    surging. . . .
Be still and know that I am God;
    I will be exalted among the nations,
    I will be exalted in the earth.
The Lord Almighty is with us;
    the God of Jacob is our fortress.
(Psalm 46:1-3, 10-11)

The storm described in verses 2 and 3 are very much like the overwhelming forces which batter us when we face the death of someone we love. But God is our refuge. He is our stability. He is mighty, and He cares deeply and passionately about us.

❏ Has your sense of identity been shaken by the death of the person you love? Explain:

❏ What other major transitions have you experienced in your lifetime? List those here, and then describe how your identity was threatened and/or shaped by each one. (In other words, in the midst of the change, did you feel unstable? After the change, what new sense of strength did you have?)

❑ Look at these passages of Scripture and describe the different aspects of your identity in Christ:
John 1:12

John 15:1-5

John 15:15

Romans 5:1

Romans 8:1

Romans 8:15

Romans 8:17

I Corinthians 3:16 and 6:19-20

II Corinthians 5:17

II Corinthians 5:18-21

Ephesians 1:3-8

Ephesians 2:5

Ephesians 2:10

Philippians 3:20

Colossians 2:13-15

Colossians 1:13-14

Colossians 2:7-13

Colossians 3:12

I Peter 2:9-10

I Peter 2:11

I John 3:1-2

I John 5:18

❑ Reflect on these passages for a few minutes, then write a summary statement of your identity in Christ.
   I am. . .

❑ Express your heart to the Lord about what you've studied.
   My Father,

Step 11

Wisdom and Understanding

Painful experiences deepen us. As we listen to the heart of God, we grow in understanding and wisdom. No, nobody would choose that path, but One has chosen it for us. And the reality is, God has chosen that path for virtually all of us at one point or another. Our culture screams at us that we should avoid pain at all costs. If we have a certain charge card, we won't have to worry about anything; if we use a certain toothpaste, we'll have lots of friends; if we use a certain investment firm, we'll have plenty of money the rest of our lives; and if we use a certain shampoo, we'll be beautiful. (I've looked in the mirror. It's going to take more than a bottle of shampoo for some of us!) Too often, we Christian's have absorbed these views, and we now believe "the abundant life" is the same as "the easy life" or "the good life." Not true.

We would learn a lot better lesson from ancient saints like St. John of the Cross or Augustine who knew that suffering was the path of growth and wisdom. Our wounds are God's preparation for imparting great truths to us, and even more importantly, imparting His heart. In a passage that communicates the exact opposite of our culture's obsession with wealth and ease, the apostle Paul wrote that we can and should actually rejoice in adversity. He wrote to the Christians in Rome: "Not only so, but we also rejoice in our sufferings, because we know that suffering produces perseverance; perseverance, character; and character, hope. And hope does not disappoint us, because God has poured out His love into our hearts by the Holy Spirit, whom he has given to us" (Romans 5:3-5).

One of the most poignant stories I've ever heard is about men who endured years of oppression, harsh work loads, and starvation in the Soviet gulags, prison camps. One man was driven to God by his experience, and day after day, year after year, the harsh conditions deepened his relationship with the Father. When he was finally released, this gaunt, shadow of a man stopped just outside the gate, knelt and wept as he kissed the stone wall. "Thank You, God," he cried, "for bringing me to this prison. Thank You, God." This man saw past the pain and realized that God was using the experience to grant him incredible blessings of intimacy, strength, and wisdom.

The great 19th century missionary to China, Hudson Taylor, said, "It doesn't matter how great the pressure is. What matters is: where does the pressure lie? Does it push you closer to God, or does it push you away from God?" All of us have pressure. The rain falls on the just and the unjust. The winds and storms blow against all houses. The question is whether we build on rocks or sand.

People who have gone through the grief process are approachable people. We are wounded, but we become, as Henri Nouwen calls us, "wounded healers" who impart the comfort to others we ourselves have experienced. One day, after months of grieving over Cindy, a woman came up to me after church and asked, "My I just hold your hand for a minute?"

I looked at her and said, "You're going through it, aren't you?"

Tears filled her eyes as she nodded. She didn't ask for great spiritual advice. She didn't want me to fix her. She just wanted to be close to someone who understood her pain.

Are we weaker because of our wounds? We are more pliable in God's hands, but that isn't the same as weakness. But in one of the many paradoxes of our faith, brokenness makes us stronger. I asked an orthopedic surgeon about the mending of broken bones, and he told me that the place where bones are broken and then regenerate is stronger than other parts of the bone. It may break again above the original break, or it may break below it, but it very rarely breaks in the same place twice. We, too, are stronger in the broken places where we've healed.

Pain is a purifier. It causes us to reevaluate our goals and priorities, and suddenly, those things that seemed so crucial before are not so important any more. The ruby of refinement leads then to the diamond of discernment. Accomplishments we were once driven to achieve don't fascinate us any more. Relationships and values we didn't make time for in the past now are the most important things in our lives. Roles as a husband and father, or mother and wife, as a disciple of Christ, and as a friend are now more important than reaching goals. When our roles take precedent over our goals and then shape our goals, we have no conflict in values because we aren't driven to achieve at any cost. And the absence of conflict in our values allows us to walk in integrity. We become more concerned about the kind of person God wants us to be than how high up some ladder we can climb. Then our secret life and our public life are consistent. Character is who you are when nobody is looking. Prayer becomes richer and deeper. Instead of going through the motions, we genuinely long to lay hold of the throne of grace and get into Abba's arms.

❑ List some commercials on television. What do these products or services promise to provide for us? What is the implicit promise of how they will give us love, acceptance, and joy?

❑ To what extent do you think you have bought into the culture's concept that "the abundant life" is equivalent to "the good life"?

❑ Are you at a stage in your grief that you feel you have "turned the corner" and you are getting stronger? Explain:

❑ Give your own definition and description of a "wounded healer":

❑ Is this attractive to you? Why or why not?

❑ Describe the people who have comforted you most during this time of grief. In what ways do they exemplify your description of "wounded healers"?

❑ Read Romans 5:3-5. Paraphrase it here:

❑ How has the grief process changed, deepened and strengthened. . .
your goals?

your values?

your relationships with family and friends?

your relationships with hurting people?

your relationship with God?

❑ Express your heart to God.
    Father, thank You for the pain I've experienced. It has. . .

Step 12

Peace and Joy

As God's Spirit works His way deep in our hearts, the confusion is gradually replaced with peace; the bitterness subsides, and joy gradually emerges. On the day Cindy died, I was sure my life was irrevocably changed for the worse. I had no possible conception that God would somehow work a miracle and use the tragedy for good in my life. In fact, I couldn't see that for many months. God used the crucible of pain to draw me near to Him and to refine my motives in the fire of grief. Before, I had gone from one goal to another, one accomplishment to the next, always looking for the next destination, focusing on the next peak and the next and the next. But God began to teach me that the journey (or "the process," as Oswald Chambers calls it), and those I am with along that journey, are infinitely more important than the destinations, no matter how high the peaks may be. He is more interested in my character than my comfort, and He will use the pain of loss—if I let Him—to transform my life.

One of the qualities I hope God has been producing in me is sincerity. Charles Swindoll wrote about the root of that word, *sincera* in Latin. The word actually means "without wax." In the days of the Roman Empire, those who made fine porcelain sometimes found cracks when they took items, such as vases, from the ovens. They developed a pearl-like wax to press into those cracks, and this wax blended in perfectly so no one would notice. But a wise buyer would hold the vase up to the sun. The translucent porcelain let the light shine through, and any wax in cracks were immediately and plainly seen. Sometimes vases were what they seemed to be; sometimes not. The valuable pieces were sincera, without wax. God wants us to be sincere, without the wax of hypocrisy to cover up the cracks in our lives. He wants us to be exactly what we seem to be: honest, forthright, with integrity. That doesn't mean we will be perfect, but we won't try to be somebody we aren't. We'll be genuine.

In my own grief experience, I learned that the faithfulness of God doesn't depend on my faithfulness. Paul reminded Timothy of one of the first hymns of the early church. In the words of that brief song, Paul reflects on the unchanging faithfulness of God. . . no matter what we do or how we respond to Him:

> If we died with him,
>   we will also live with him;
> if we endure,
>   we will also reign with him.
> If we disown him,
>   he will also disown us;
> if we are faithless,
>   he will remain faithful,
>   for he cannot disown himself
> (II Timothy 2:11-13)

I learned to trust God, not in theory, but in actual experience. It's one thing to talk about trusting Him, but it's another thing to know you're going to die emotionally and spiritually if He doesn't come through. I simply couldn't have lived if God had not met me in the deepest pit of my despair. But he did. I am reminded of something Corrie ten Boom said about her experience at Ravensbrook Nazi concentration camp. She was talking with her sister who questioned how God could be real to them in such a horrible place. Corrie responded, "There is no pit so deep that God is not deeper still." My situation is not the same as theirs, but I had the same doubts as Corrie's sister. I learned, as Corrie said, that no matter how deep the hole is for you and me, God is deeper still.

A part of the joy I find now is that I am able to help others who grieve. I hope I helped them before, but I'm much more understanding of their needs now that I have experienced those same needs. I realize in a new and fuller way the power of prayer. It's so easy to say, "I'll pray for you," and shoot up a perfunctory prayer or forget altogether. But there was a time after Cindy died that my life, whether I could go forward or slipped back into despair, depended on the prayers of faithful friends. If it hadn't been for them lifting me to the Father, I shudder to think where I'd be today.

The grief process is not a straight, clear path. It involves twists and turns, ups and downs, moving forward and sliding backward. Perhaps you have already made great progress over a long period of time, and you are sensing the wisdom, understanding, peace and joy I've described in these last two steps. Or maybe you are not that far along yet. That's okay. Just be assured that healing will come. It takes time and attention to overcome the blows you've experienced, and it takes the hand of God to lead you through. Sometimes God will deliver us *from* the fire, but sometimes He delivers us *through* the fire.

Many times in the Scriptures we are encouraged to "wait for the Lord." We usually think of waiting only in terms of time, but the Bible uses that term to indicate a heart of trusting anticipation, like you are waiting for your friend (who would never forget) to pick you up. In this waiting, we have great confidence in the outcome. Psalm 27 is a beautiful psalm of trust in God. It ends with David's encouragement:

> I am confident of this:
>   I will see the goodness of the Lord
>   in the land of the living.
> Wait for the Lord;
>   be strong and take heart
>   and wait for the Lord
> (Psalm 27:13-14)

Dear friend, I hope this book and workbook has seemed like I was there with you as you read and reflected in these pages. I trust you are sensing the nearness of God as He comforts your heart and gives you strength and insight. I encourage you to continue to go to your group and talk to your partner as long as you feel the need, for years if that is what helps you. Many people find it encouraging to go through this workbook two or three times over a period of many months. Some things that they failed to understand and apply the first time become clearer as they continue to make progress in their healing journey.

And keep trusting God's heart, even when you can't trace His hand.

❑ How have you seen God's faithfulness in your life over these months?

❑ Describe how suffering can help you become more sincere, "without wax":

❑ Have you found Corrie ten Boom's statement to be true: "There is no pit so deep that God is not deeper still." Why or why not?

❑ Read Psalm 27:13-14. What does it mean to you to "wait for the Lord"?

❑ How has God used you to comfort other grieving people?

❑ What is the next step for you in your journey? What do you need to keep going and growing?

Appendix A

How to be a Grief Partner

It is a high honor to be asked to be a grief partner. The person you help is at a very needy spot in his or her life, and that person has chosen you (or perhaps your pastor has chosen you) to minister the grace and strength of God to that person's broken heart. I've heard it said that a definition of a friend is "someone who walks in the room when everybody else is walking out." That's not a value judgment on those who walk away from needy people. Perhaps they want to help but they don't know how. Maybe they are struggling with their own problems and are too preoccupied to help. Yours is a great honor—and a great responsibility—to walk hand-in-hand with a wounded person in grief.

I want to identify several characteristics that are important for you as a grief partner:

1. Supervised—If your church has a formal grief support ministry, there is probably someone who supervises the partners (or sponsors or whatever they are called in your church). The supervisor may be one of the pastors, a counselor, or someone who has been in the grief ministry for a long time and is skilled at shepherding those who help people in grief.

If your church doesn't have a formal ministry like this and you want to be a partner, ask a skilled counselor or pastor to be your supervisor. From time to time, you will have questions you need answered. You may encounter explosive emotions that you don't know how to handle, or the person you are helping may show signs of clinical depression. It is wise to have someone you can call to get the assistance you need.

2. Training—Your church may have a lay counselor training program to equip those who are involved in all

aspects of the counseling ministry: grief, codependency, chemical dependency, sexual abuse, eating disorders, etc. These training programs will add insight and understanding so you will be ready for many different situations as you help people.

3. Experience—We cannot take someone down a path we have not traveled ourselves. That doesn't mean you have to experience the exact same loss to effectively help a grieving person, but you need to have gone through the grieving process in some way yourself. Your life experience will make you more empathetic, and it will enable you to anticipate the person's needs at each step in the process. Your own healing experiences will enable you to be authentic and share out of the wealth of your own hurts and hope.

4. Trust God for wisdom—Helping people is a spiritual experience. No matter how much training and experience we have, we need God to guide us. Pray for God to give you His heart for that person, His wisdom for direction, and His insight to share with that person.

A part of the wisdom God gives us (and indeed, He has already given us) is to pair partners with same sex individuals who are grieving: men with men, women with women. The depth of people's needs, and the necessary outpouring of emotions during this time make it vital that we don't add any possibility of transferring affections.

5. Listen—And listen some more! In most conversations, people interrupt within 60 seconds. Let the person talk without correcting her. There will be time to give feedback later. Ask the second and third questions to draw the person out and go deeper into the well of insight. And listen with your eyes. Look for any dissonance between the person's words and his facial expressions and tone of voice. For instance, if someone says, "I feel so bad today. I'm hopeless," but she is smiling, then she probably feels very uncomfortable telling you her feelings. That is a signal she needs an extra measure of love and care.

Watch, too, for the person's body language to get a picture of what's going on inside.

Give eye contact to let the person know you are there—really there—for him. Your own body language, facial expressions, and tone of voice will indicate if you are in a hurry to get the appointment over so you can get to more important things, or if you really care.

From time to time, reflect back what the person has said to clarify points for both of you: "What I'm hearing you say is. . . ." The person may say, "Yes, that's how I feel," but she may say, "No, that's not it at all!" Reflecting is a benchmark for good communication between you.

6. Availability—If you only have one hour a week at a given time for someone, this may not be the time for you to be a grief partner. On the other hand, you don't want to get into a codependent relationship in which a needy person is depending on you to meet every need. There must be balance. And there must be clear expectations up front on both sides.

When the partnership begins, ask, "What are your expectations of our relationship?" Establish ground rules of how much time you spend together, how late at night are phone calls acceptable, and what the checkpoints are in the relationship to be sure it stays on track. The supervisor will give you clear guidelines about realistic expectations.

Accountability is an important part of any sponsor or partner relationship, but here again, the expectations need to be clearly defined at appropriate points. In the earliest days, a friendship is probably what is needed. Later, when the grind of the grief process makes it important for the person to set specific recovery goals, it is appropriate to ask the grieving person about progress on particular goals from week to week.

7. Confidentiality—Never violate a person's trust, or he may not open up to anyone again for a long, long time. Whatever the person tells you, keep it in strictest confidence so he will fell safe to bare his soul and share his deepest hurts, anger, and confusion. An exception to this

is if you think there is a risk of homicidal or suicidal behavior. Then you are required to tell your supervisor immediately. Your supervisor will ask you questions from time to time about the person's progress. This, too, is a confidential relationship, so you can share (with that person alone, not in a group) specifics of the relationship. Even then, you may want to veil the specifics and share only general information. The reporting procedure should be discussed and decided between you and your supervisor during the training process.

8. Referral—Sometimes a person's needs are simply beyond our skill level. In that case, we need to refer the person to a doctor or counselor. Talk to your supervisor or pastor about the most suitable referral, and help the person make contact. But stay involved with the hurting person so she won't feel abandoned by you.

9. Group involvement—One of the most powerful and positive situations is for partnerships to take place in the context of a grief support group. In the vast majority of cases, the combination of one-on-one partnership and group involvement encourages reflection, honest, and growth better than either would do alone.

10. Help that person become a partner—As the person you are helping gets stronger, she may want to help others, too. At first, this assistance will necessarily be unstructured. Perhaps she will encourage others in the group or wounded individuals in the church. As months and years pass, the desire may grow to be in a more formal position as a grief partner. This once deeply wounded person will then see God use the wisdom, compassion, and strength she has gained in a ministry to other wounded people.

If you want your church to begin or expand a grief ministry, talk to your pastor to see what needs to be done. Show the staff this section of the book which they can use as a template to design this ministry, and pray for them as they make decisions about it. If they have questions, have them contact a professional counselor or a the leader of a grief ministry in another church for advice and direction.

Appendix B

How to Lead a Grief Support Group

Support groups are environments of grace for hurting people. Your church may already have these groups for people who struggle with chemical dependency, codependency, or addictions to food, sex, or work. The church may also have a group for victims of sexual abuse. A grief support group does not target those with addictions or the victims of abuse, so the dynamics are somewhat different. For instance, those who attend a grief group may not struggle with long-term, family or origin problems that are addressed in these other groups.

Here are some things to consider as you plan for a grief support group:

1. Class vs. group—Some churches and some communities conduct classes for people who have lost loved ones. People are invited to a weekend seminar or a series for several weeks at which a counselor or author communicates principles to help people deal with their loss. These classes are valuable and provide much-needed input. A group, however, focuses more on relationships and support than on content. The group time is spent usually allowing members to share their hurts and struggles so others in the group can come alongside and encourage them. There may be, of course, some content communicated, but the primary reason to be there is the loving support for one another.

2. Open vs. closed groups—Open groups welcome new members at any time. Closed groups typically allow new members for a couple of weeks, then they are closed to newcomers for some period of time, usually about three months. There are benefits and liabilities of each. People don't schedule when they need to grieve. They need a group the day they feel the need to go to get help. On the

other hand, closed groups generally build trust and intimacy more quickly because members don't have the instability of wondering if new people are trustworthy. I've seen both types of groups work very well. If you choose to have a closed group, you can use partners to meet with people until the group is open again.

3. Ongoing vs specific time—Ongoing groups give people a sense of strength and patience because they know the group will be there whenever they need it. A 13-week group usually goes in cycles: it starts again after each 13-week series ends. These groups often have specific content (like this book and workbook), but content can also be used effectively in an ongoing group. Both types can work well. The choice depends on the group leader or the supervisor of grief groups.

4. Dynamics of a group—
● Love and acceptance
     When we take time to listen, we communicate concern and love. When we hug someone who feels down, we let them know they are not alone. When we share our own struggles, we make it safe for others to be honest about their hurts, too. Don't feel that you have to be the "Answer Man" who solves every problem immediately with a word of wisdom. Listen carefully to people as they talk. Look at them. Ask them second and third follow up questions to continue to draw them out. That will communicate that you really care about them. Also, use the ointment of thankfulness liberally. Say things like, "Thanks for telling us about your problem." Or "That took courage for you to tell us. Can we pray for you right now?" If someone shares something which needs your private attention, you can say, "Thank you for trusting us enough to tell us. Let's talk more about it after the meeting." Your kindness and attention give you the platform to speak the truth to receptive hearts.
● Trust
     Appropriate self-disclosure is one of the best ways to build a trustworthy environment. When you tell stories about your own failures, successes, hurts, fears, and

hopes, others readily identify with you. Be careful, however, not to tell too much or tell it too graphically. For instance, you don't want to tell the intimate details of your sins, and it is inappropriate to tell the names of others who acted inappropriately in your stories, especially if the listeners might know those people. Use self-disclosing statements such as, "I felt . . . when my father died."

Encourage others to talk about their dreams and dreads, too. As people feel safe, they will see how the truth you communicate applies to these areas of their lives. If someone shares about a particularly explosive family situation, however, it may be appropriate to gently interrupt and say, "Thank you so much for telling us about your hurts. I'm sure many people in here can identify with you. I'd like to talk more with you after the meeting. Do you have a few minutes to talk to me then?"

● Information

People are looking for "handles on the truth" so they can apply it to their relationships and experiences. As you teach, use quotes from books, the newspaper, and periodicals to add "punch" to your group meetings. Personal illustrations or stories of others' experiences paint word pictures for listeners.

The Bible can seem very dull and boring when it's compared to the excitement of today's videos and movies. And too often, we who teach the Bible contribute to this perception because we don't make these life-changing truths understandable or relevant to our listeners. Help people identify with the truth of the Scriptures by asking them open questions such as, "How would you have felt in this situation? What would you have done?" Or "What would Jesus do in this situation if He were here today?" Invite them to respond, but you don't need to comment on the validity of each response. Simply thank each person for his contribution and summarize at the end.

● Hope

Your group's environment of love, trust, and truth provides hope and encouragement. Think of times when you felt confused and discouraged. When someone believed in you, you probably felt both surprised and strengthened! Grieving people need to be reminded that the Lord is strong and loving. He loves them deeply and desires their best. Though they may not understand their situations, He does.

Group leaders have the privilege of giving hope to these needy people:

—In the face of confusion, we can encourage them to make good decisions.

—In the face of weakness, we can help them to be strong.

—In the face of despair, we can tell them there is life on the other side of the present problem.

—In the face of guilt, we can share the forgiveness of Jesus Christ.

—In the face of bitterness, we can teach them to forgive others.

Be careful, however, not to over-promise! The Lord never promised to protect His children from all problems or bail them out. He promised to be with us in the middle of our struggles and to give us wisdom and strength to do His will.

● Limitations

Though support groups encourage a deep level of openness and vulnerability, there are limits to a leader's training and time to be able to deal effectively with the problems which surface. Some mistakenly think that they need to resolve every problem which surfaces in the group, but this overwhelming sense of responsibility leads to burn-out for the leader as he is driven to fix the problems in many people's lives, or in contrast, it can lead to a denial that there are any significant problems at all. Neither of these is productive.

Before problems arise, be aware of the limits of your training, skills, and time to be able to deal with complex individual and family problems which people bring up in the group.

I strongly recommend that you develop relationships with competent counselors and agencies in the community instead of playing a counselor's role yourself. These professionals are trained to handle the complex and dynamic struggles in individuals and families. You can request to be informed of progress when a person is referred. Be sure, however, to do your homework so you know the expertise and spiritual persuasion of the person to whom you refer someone.

● Scheduling

If you choose to use this book in a 13-week series, I recommend:

—Use the first meeting to communicate the goals of the group, introduce people, and acquaint people with the material. Have enough copies of the book available for each person to buy one.

—Each of the next 12 weeks will cover a chapter each week. Of course, it is impossible to fully discuss each point in this short amount of time, so be sensitive to the need for people to talk. You may need to schedule another 13-week series or an on-going group for those who want more depth. The last meeting of the series can be a recap of what has been learned and a discussion of what the group wants to do next. They may choose to disband the group, they may choose to continue, or they may split up into two or more groups.

5. Partners—

Partners (or sponsors) give one-on-one care to group members and strengthen the leadership of the group. It is not necessary for each partner to attend the group, but that is desirable. (See Appendix A for more information about partners.)

6. Beginning the group—

● First, meet with your pastor or staff to share information and plan for the group. You will want to discuss the issues in this appendix to make sure you are in agreement about the objectives of the group and how it will be conducted. You will also want to plan on how the group will be made known in the church, and possibly, in the community. Other issues to address are:

—who will lead the group

—content and materials

—who pays for the materials, the group members or the church?

—closed or open?
—ongoing or specific time?
—where the group will meet
—supervisors and partners
—meeting time and place
—child care
—refreshments
—referral sources
—the reporting procedure (accountability of the leader to the pastor or staff)
•Select and train the group leader and partners
•Plan and schedule the publicity about the group, including:
—a bulletin announcement
—an announcement from the pulpit
—announcements in Sunday school classes and other gatherings
—posters in the community (if desired)
•You may also contact specific people to invite them to come to the group.
•Begin the group by having enough books available, refreshments, comfortable seating, and child care, if possible.
(This Group Leader's Guide was adapted from *Rapha's Handbook for Group Leaders*, Richard Price and Pat Springle, (Rapha: Houston, 1992), pp. 51-64.)

Appendix C
Some of the Bible's Best Words for Those Who Mourn

"But He knows the way that I take;
When He has tested me, I shall come forth as gold"
(Job 23:10).

"For the LORD has heard the voice of my weeping.
The LORD has heard my supplication;
The LORD will receive my prayer" (Psalm 6:8-9).

"Weeping may endure for a night,
But joy comes in the morning" (Psalm 30:5).

"Commit your way to the LORD,
Trust also in Him,
And He shall bring it to pass" (Psalm 37:5).

"Rest in the LORD, and wait patiently for Him"
(Psalm 37:5).

"God is our refuge and strength,
A very present help in trouble" (Psalm 46:1).

"Cast your burden on the LORD,
And He shall sustain you" (Psalm 55:22).

"For He shall give His angels charge over you,
To keep you in all your ways" (Psalm 91:11).

"He heals the broken-hearted,
And binds up their wounds" (Psalm 147:3).

"Trust in the LORD with all your heart,
And lean not on your own understanding;
In all your ways acknowledge Him,
And He shall direct your paths" (Proverbs 3:5, 6).

"But those who wait on the LORD Shall renew their
  strength;
They shall mount up with wings like eagles,
They shall run and not be weary,
They shall walk and not faint" (Isaiah 40:31).

"When you pass through the waters, I will be with you;
And through the rivers, they shall not overflow you.
When you walk through the fire, you shall not be burned,
Nor shall the flame scorch you. For I am the LORD you
  God. . . .
Fear not, for I am with you" (Isaiah 43:2-3, 5).

"I am the resurrection and the life. He who believes in
Me, though he may die, he shall live. And whoever lives
and believes in Me shall never die" (John 11:25, 26).

"Let not your heart be troubled; you believe in God,
believe also in Me. In My Father's house are many
mansions; if it were not so, I would have told you. I go to
prepare a place for you. And if I go and prepare a place
for you, I will come again and receive you to Myself; that
where I am, there you may be also" (John 14:1-3).

"Peace I leave with you, My peace I give to you; not as the
world gives do I give to you. Let not your heart be
troubled, neither let it be afraid" (John 14:27).

"Likewise the Spirit also helps in our weaknesses. For
we do not know what we should pray for as we ought, but
the Spirit Himself makes intercession for us with
groanings which cannot be uttered" (Romans 8:26).

"For He Himself has said, 'I will never leave you nor forsake you.' So we may boldly say: 'The LORD is my helper'" (Hebrews 13:5, 6).

"My brethren, count it all joy when you fall into various trials, knowing that the testing of your faith produces patience. But let patience have its perfect work, that you may be perfect and complete, lacking nothing" (James 1:2-5).

"And I heard a loud voice from heaven saying, 'Behold, the tabernacle of God is with men, and He will dwell with them, and they shall be His people, and God Himself will be with them and be their God. And God will wipe away every tear from their eyes; there shall be no more death, nor sorrow, nor crying; and there shall be no more pain, for the former things have passed away'" (Revelation 21:3, 4).

If You Want to Trust Christ

As you have read this book, perhaps the Lord has awakened faith in your heart, and you want to trust Christ as your Savior. The angels rejoice, and so do I!

God is trustworthy. He said He would forgive your sins and make you His own dear child. To experience His grace, pray this prayer. It's as simple as A-B-C.

Acknowledge Jesus Christ is the One who loves you
  enough to die for you. He is God, Savior, and Friend.
Believe in Christ as your Savior.
Confess your sin, and confess Jesus as your Lord.

You can pray something like this:
Lord Jesus, I acknowledge that You died to pay for my sins. Right now, I accept Your death on the cross as the full payment for all my sins. Thank You for forgiving me, and thank You for giving me eternal life. You are my Savior, and You are my Lord. Amen.

As a child of God, your sins are forgiven, the Holy Spirit lives in you, and you will spend eternity in heaven with your loving Heavenly Father. I want to encourage you by providing some information for you. Please write me at:

NorthStar Church
P.O. Box 2349
Kennesaw, Georgia 30144

I'll send you some materials to help you grow in your faith, and I'll be praying for you, too! If you ever get near Kennesaw, Georgia, come visit us at Northstar Church. We'd love to have you!

Notes

Chapter 8
1. C. S. Lewis, *A Grief Observed,* (New York: Bantam Books, 1961), 80-81.

Chapter 10
1. Eugenia Price, *Getting Through the Night,* (New York: Dial Press, 1982), 4.

Chapter12
1. Price, *Getting Through the Night,* 34.

Chapter 16
1. Annie Johnson Flint, "He Giveth More Grace," 1941. Renewed 1969 by Lillenas Publishing Co. All rights reserved. Used by permission.

Chapter 17
1. Jacob M. Braude, *Complete Speaker's and Toastmaster's Library,* (Englewood Clifts, NJ: Prentice-Hall), 47.

Chapter18
1. Billy Graham, *Angels—God's Secret Agents,* (Garden City, NY: Doubleday, 1975) 149.
2. Jordan C. Khan, in *Topical Encyclopedia of Living Quotations,* Sherwood Eliot Wirt and Kersten Beckstrom (Minneapolis: Bethany House, 1982), 106.

Chapter19
1. John Powell, *Why Am I Afraid to Love?,* (Niles, IL: Argus Communications, 1967, rev. 1972), 29.
2. Henry Drummond, in *Inspiring Quotations,* Albert M. Wells, Jr. (Nashville: Thomas Nelson, 1988), 1564.

Chapter 20
1. Melba Cosgrove, Harold H. Bloomfield, Peter
    McWilliams, *How to Survive the Loss of a Love,*
    (New York: Bantam Books, 1976), 64.

Chapter 21
1. See Frank B. Minirth and Paul D. Meier, *Happiness
    Is a Choice,* (Grand Rapids, MI: Baker, 1978), 111ff.

Chapter 22
1. John H. Yates, "Faith is the Victory," *Hymns For the
    Family of God,* (Nashville: Paragon Associates, 1976),
    hymn 12.
2. Gordon MacDonald, *Renewing Your Spiritual
    Passion,* (Nashville: Thomas Nelson, 1986), 126.

Chapter 23
1. C. S. Lewis, *A Grief Observed,* (New York: Bantam
    Books by arrangement with Seabury Press, 1976)
2. John Powell, *Fully Human, Fully Alive,* (Niles, IL:
    Argus Communications, 1976), 7.

About The Author

Dwight "Ike" Reighard is pastor of NorthStar Church in Kennesaw, Georgia. He has a wide and diverse speaking and preaching ministry which includes inspirational, motivational, and evangelistic topics, as well as subjects dealing with church growth and youth work. Aside from his extensive ministry to adults, he speaks to throngs of teenagers annually.

He received a B. A. in religion (Magna Cum Laude) from Mercer University, a Master of Divinity from Luther Rice Seminary, a Doctor of Ministry from Luther Rice, and an Honorary Doctor of Literature from Southern California Theological Seminary.

He served as president of the Georgia Baptist Convention and is currently on the boards of several universities and other organizations, such as Liberty University, Rapha Treatment Centers, Alpha Care, and Psychological Studies Institute at Georgia State.

Dr. Reighard and his wife, Robin, have two daughters, Abigail and Danielle, and reside in Powder Springs, Georgia.

For More Information About:

Materials:
—Additional copies of *Treasures from the Dark*
—Ike Reighard's tape series:
  - "Stepping Stones to Success"
  - "Creating Championship Character in Your Child"
  - "8 Secrets of Happiness"

Seminars:
—**Church seminars**
  - Ike Reighard, **Treasures from the Dark**
    Helping people learn to grieve
  - Ike Reighard, **NorthStar**
    Determining what God wants you to do with your life, and
    pursuing it with vision and a clear plan of action
—**Business seminars**
  - Ike Reighard, **Filing a Flight Plan for Your Life**
    Getting a vision and plan for your life and business
  - James D. Murphy, **After Burner**
    Business is combat—learn task saturation and team building
  - Jay Strack, **What Retailers Want to Know about the Millennial Generation**
    Recruiting, training, and supervising today's teenagers
  - Jay Strack, **How to Market to the Millennial Generation**
    Sell more products by knowing their wants and meeting
    their needs
  - Lt. Col. William "Buck" Burney, **The Mission of Life**
    Establishing personal goals and values

For prices and scheduling, contact us by:
Phone. . . (888) 242-5325
Mail. . . Quantum Leap Productions
          576 Delphinium Blvd. Ste 100
          Acworth, GA 30102
E-mail. . . QuantumProductions.com